Praise for

Conversational
INTELLIGENCE
and **Judith E. Glaser**

"Before you can persuade others, you need to know how to listen and how to communicate. With the best of intentions, we can fall back into patterns and old habits that are less than ideal—it's just the way we're wired. *Conversational Intelligence* builds on the fundamental science of communication to help you achieve more attunement with others. If you're not getting the results you want, maybe it's time to give your 'C-IQ' a boost."

—Daniel H. Pink, best-selling author of
Drive and *To Sell Is Human*

"Drawing on a lifetime of […] advising America's top executives, Judith Glaser delivers a masterful analysis of the power of conversation, sharing countless examples of how business leaders are driving change and achieving superior results by leveraging the art and science of 'Conversational Intelligence' strategies."

—Kathryn A. Tesija, executive vice president,
Merchandising and Supply Chain for Target

"If each of us used and embodied the principles of *Conversational Intelligence* conveyed by Glaser in this book, it would not only create winning outcomes for businesses, it would change the world! This is a must-read for anyone who wants to have major impact in the world, and especially for those in leadership. The concept of Level III Conversation is a total game changer!"

—Jane Stevenson, vice chairman of Board &
CEO Services of Korn/Ferry International,
and co-author of the best-seller, *Breaking Away: How Great Leaders Create Innovation that Drives Sustainable Growth and Why Others Fail*

"Judith Glaser's new book, *Conversational Intelligence*, encapsulates the importance of transparency when building respectful relationships that are founded on mutual understanding. In my organization, radical transparency is a core tenet of our business. Glaser's method supports our practiced philosophy of transparency, but boils it down to the conversational level, making this a practical guide for individual employees, teams, leaders and organizations to work toward mutually agreed upon success."

—Ryan Smith, co-founder and CEO of Qualtrics, contributor to *The Wall Street Journal*, and named one of *Forbes'* "America's Most Promising CEOs Under 35" for 2013

"In her new book, *Conversational Intelligence*, Judith Glaser provides tools that help understand what is going on in our conversations with one another and how to elevate our 'Conversational Intelligence.' Conversations that facilitate connectivity with others enable us to activate our higher executive functions to help build common goals throughout an organization. *Conversational Intelligence* is a must-read for everyone in an organization driving for high quality relationships, shared success and strengthening the organization's ability to make good decisions."

—Alessa Quane, chief risk officer, AIG

"Words are the ideas on which change is built — if we can see the world we want, we need to learn to express that vision in ways that engage others to join our movement and make it a reality. *Conversational Intelligence* is crucial for that to happen!"

—Caryl Stern, president and CEO, U.S. Fund for UNICEF and author of *I Believe in Zero: Learning from the World's Children*

"So, you think you have the gift of gab? That you're an experienced communicator and it's served you well in your career? Think again. Great communication, rather than being a programmed trait, is actually a hard-won skill, and learning how to communicate well requires a master guide. Now we have one. Judith Glaser, an internationally respected executive coach and consultant, has broken the mold with her latest book, *Conversational Intelligence*. . . . Simply said, this book is a find."

—Jon Entine, executive director of the Genetic
Literacy Project, George Mason University
and author of *Taboo* and *Abraham's Children*

"In modern-day businesses that operate across continents, cultures, or vast generational differences, a mere turn of phrase can mean conflict, chaos, and wasted resources. Glaser's new book, *Conversational Intelligence*, will help leaders at all levels learn to engage their heads and hearts to generate trusting relationships that drive their companies to being really great local and global players."

—The Honorable Mary K. Bush, president of
Bush International, LLC and senior managing director
of Brock Capital Group, LLC

"In a world with increasingly more information with often less relevance, Judith Glaser has written a primer on taking our daily conversations from typically superficial transactions to meaningful ones in an effort to transform the world around us. Using neuroscience, social science research, and a dose of folk wisdom, *Conversational Intelligence* presents models, tools, and examples relevant to enhancing any part of our professional and personal communication lives."

—Sandra L. Shullman, PhD, managing partner of
Executive Development Group, LLC

"In my experience there are books that stimulate the mind, there are books that inspire the heart, and there are books that give practical tools for application. However, it is rare when you find a book that accomplishes all three. *Conversational Intelligence* is one of those rare books. Judith Glaser's wisdom and insight draw the reader into the 'heart' of her message: *'To get to the next level of greatness depends on the quality of the culture, which depends on the quality of relationships, which depends on the quality of conversations. Everything happens through conversations.'*"

—Michael J. Stabile, Ph.D., clinical professor in the Department of Educational Leadership and Human Resource Development, Xavier University, and founder and president of FutureNow Consulting, LLC

"Judith Glaser's years of study and experience as an executive coach in large companies have brought her profound insights that manifest themselves in this book of effective strategies underpinned by science and the wisdom of her own heart. Every executive, manager, and coach can benefit from understanding and developing *Conversational Intelligence*."

—Deborah Rozman, Ph.D., and CEO of Institute of HeartMath

Conversational
INTELLIGENCE

Conversational
INTELLIGENCE

*How Great
Leaders*
BUILD TRUST
*and Get
Extraordinary
Results*

JUDITH E. GLASER

bibliomotion
books + media

First published by Bibliomotion, Inc.
711 Third Avenue, New York, NY 10017, USA
2 Park Square, Milton Park, Abingdon, Oxon OX14 4RN, UK

Bibliomotion is an imprint of the Taylor & Francis Group, an informa business

First Paperback Edition ISBN 978-1-62956-143-1

The Library of Congress has cataloged the hardcover edition as follows:

Library of Congress Cataloging-in-Publication Data

Glaser, Judith E.
   Conversational intelligence : how great leaders build trust & get extraordinary results / by Judith E. Glaser.
     pages cm
   ISBN 978-1-937134-67-9 (hardback) — ISBN 978-1-937134-68-6 (ebook) — ISBN 978-1-937134-69-3 (enhanced ebook)
   1. Communication in management—Psychological aspects.   2. Conversation—Psychological aspects.   3. Emotional intelligence.   4. Interpersonal communication.
5. Organizational behavior.   6. Management—Psychological aspects.   7. Leadership—Psychological aspects.   I. Title.
   HD30.3.G57 2013
   650.101'4—dc23

                              2013020748

Conversational Intelligence *is dedicated to my family ... my husband Richard, my "favorite" children Rebecca, and Jacob; to my sister Joan Heffler, and my brother Jon Entine; who have all taught me how important family bonds really are, and how important it is to "stay in the conversation" even when it becomes difficult.*

CONTENTS

Introduction   Discovering a New Intelligence   xiii

PART I   Conversational Intelligence and Why We Need It

 1 What We Can Learn from Our Worst Conversations   3

 2 When We Lose Trust, We Lose Our Voice   21

 3 Moving from Distrust to Trust   33

PART II   Raising Your Conversational Intelligence

 4 Challenges of Navigating the Conversational Highway   61

 5 Harvesting Conversational Intelligence Using the Wisdom
   of Our Five Brains   73

 6 Bringing Conversations to Life   87

 7 Priming for Level III Conversations   101

 8 Conversational Agility: Reframing, Refocusing, Redirecting   117

 9 A Toolkit for Level III Conversations   137

Contents

PART III   Getting to the Next Level of Greatness

10 Leading with Trust: Laying the Foundation for
Level III Interactions   153

11 Teaming Up Through Conversational Intelligence   167

12 Changing the Game Through Conversational Intelligence   183

Epilogue   Creating Conversations That Change the World   201

Endnotes   207

References   211

Acknowledgments   213

Index   223

INTRODUCTION

Discovering a New Intelligence

You never change things by fighting the existing reality. To change something, build a new model that makes the existing model obsolete.

—BUCKMINSTER FULLER

Conversations are not what we think they are. We've grown up with a narrow view of conversations, thinking they are about talking, sharing information, telling people what to do, or telling others what's on our minds. We are now learning, through neurological and cognitive research, that a "conversation" goes deeper and is more robust than simple information sharing. Conversations are dynamic, interactive, and inclusive. They evolve and impact the way we connect, engage, interact, and influence others, enabling us to shape reality, mind-sets, events, and outcomes in a collaborative way. Conversations have the power to move us from "power-over" others to "power-with" others, giving us the exquisite ability to get on the same page with our fellow humans and experience the same reality by bridging the reality gaps between "how you see things and how I see things."[1]

Conversational Intelligence® is what separates those who are successful from those who are not—in business, in relationships, and even in marriages. For more than a half a century I've studied conversations and their impact.

Introduction

My passion to make sense of conversations was launched at a young age, and has propelled me forward into research, writing, and consulting that drives my waking and sleeping moments. Without healthy conversations we shrivel up and die—that is what we are now learning from the world of neuroscience. In fact, we now have mounting evidence that "our brain physically shrivels up and dies."

For example, a six-year study by researchers at the University of Wisconsin–Madison found convincing evidence that growing up in severe poverty affects the way children's brains develop, potentially putting them at a lifelong disadvantage. The study drew on 823 magnetic resonance images (MRI), scans of 389 children, ages four to twenty-two, from a National Institutes of Health study done to show normal brain development. The scans were done from November 2001 to August 2007, and the NIH study included complete information on the families' social and economic status.[2]

What was most stunning about the research is that the researchers were able to identify the parts of the brain that are at risk. That children who grow up in poverty do less well in school is well documented. But studies increasingly show that at least part of that overall poor performance stems from how their brains grow and work.

The University of Wisconsin study estimated that as much as 20 percent of the gap in test scores could be explained by slower development of two parts of the brain: the frontal lobe and the temporal lobe. The frontal lobe is important for controlling attention, inhibition, emotions, and complex learning. The temporal lobe is important for memory and language comprehension, such as identifying and attaching meaning to words.

Our thirty years of hands on experiments and tracking clients for years after our interventions through Benchmark Communications, Inc. and also through our CreatingWE Institutes—a division of Benchmark Communications, Inc.—has revealed that healthy conversations between parents and children can lay a dramatically better growth trajectory for children, even those who live in poverty. Healthy conversations are the game changer!

Research like the longitudinal studies from the University of Wisconsin, and Michigan,provide examples of why my commitment to bringing Conversational Intelligence (C-IQ) to business, universities, schools, and families gets stronger every day.[3] Research fuels the urgency and my passion fuels the journey.

Since Conversational Intelligence was launched in October 2013, we've been receiving extraordinary feedback from people around the world expressing their gratitude to me for writing and sharing *Conversational Intelligence: How Great Leaders Build Trust and Get Extraordinary Results.*

Because of such great curiosity and interest, I have been asked to write blog posts for media outlets such as the *Harvard Business Review,* the *Huffington Post, Psychology Today, Entrepreneur* magazine, the *Times of India, HBR* Russian edition, *C-Suite,* and more. On the broadcast side, I was invited to appear on *CBS This Morning* with Charlie Rose and Gayle King to talk about Conversational Intelligence—it was an honor and privilege, and an experience I will never forget. Subsequently, they invited me back to talk about "Being Addicted to Being Right" and many other topics that focus on core C-IQ ideas and principles.

New companies are contacting the CreatingWE Institute, requesting that we work with them to bring Conversational Intelligence to their companies globally. What is most extraordinary is why and how they want their employees to be exposed to these new frameworks and disciplines. Companies are saying they want to "graft" Conversational Intelligence into their organizations in multiple ways in order to activate a new and healthier "chemistry of conversations" in the workplace. This means they see that C-IQ is not just a training program—it's a platform that introduces new rituals and a new language for change that appeals to people throughout the company. One of my big clients called it "situation agnostic," meaning C-IQ applies to all interaction dynamics at all levels of a company, and creates a shared language for elevating everyone at the same time. One client said, "C-IQ is so simple to understand and even easier to bring to a company without resistance and with enthusiasm." Another noted, "After we experimented with some of the Conversational Rituals, we got such great feedback, people asked for more! The demand came from people seeing the value and inviting others to join them in learning how to raise the quality of the conversations throughout the company."

As a result of the high demand for companies around the globe to certify their organizations in Conversational Intelligence, we have launched CreatingWE Institutes in different parts of the world, setting them up as Centers of Excellence that will enable others to facilitate and teach our work. (See creatingwe.com.) This is a huge step forward in ensuring that we have highly talented and skilled consultants equipped to take this work forward in the best way possible.

Over the past two years, the level of client interest has soared, and includes companies in the Fortune 50 as well as entrepreneurial companies that want to create a culture of innovation and collaboration using Conversational Intelligence as the vehicle. The word is spreading from companies to countries, and to news journalists who are contacting us to be interviewed about how Conversational Intelligence can be a facilitator in government, in the development of country cultures, in early and advanced education, and more.

One of our largest and most exciting projects, launching in 2016, is a partnership with WBECS (World Business Executive Coaching Summits), founded by Ben Croft. With Ben's talented organization, we launched the first ever program in Conversational Intelligence for Coaches, which is bringing our approaches, frameworks, and tools to coaches in more than 149 countries so they can amplify and elevate their existing approaches with our transformational work.

When we launched Conversational Intelligence for Coaches we started with a complimentary webinar—and were prepared to run three sessions—with 1,000 people per session. Beyond our wildest imaginations, we ended up having to open up eight sessions and had 12,500 people attend. We have continued with just under 1,000 people who signed up for our year-long program leading to a certification for 300 coaches who will be elevated to working with us to bring C-IQ to companies and countries.

This is the largest program we have launched ever, and because of popular demand, we have already started planning for 2017 and beyond. I was surprised to learn WBECS wanted to focus on C-IQ, with all of the incredible thought leaders' work they could have drawn from for an in-depth program. Later I learned that in both 2014 and 2015 my two webinars through the WBECS Summit garnered the highest ratings from the coaches who participated. I was astounded and thrilled—and extremely excited about partnering with Ben and his absolutely incredible team including Lisa Knox, program director, Jennifer Mansell program coordinator, and a dozen other amazingly talented designers and technical gurus. Most of all, I brought into our project three amazing colleagues—Tracy Quinton and Rebecca Hahn—who worked with me in developing the Global Coach Certification program and Anna Berzitskaya, my chief of staff, who helped bring this program to life.

For a program this big and expansive we needed to cultivate more extraordinary talent, and I brought in Rhonda York, who has worked with me on developing C-IQ for the past decade, and Mary Ann Somerville who has helped bring C-IQ to the world through her incredible teaching and certification programs. Another great consultant who joined our team is Barb Girson, who is helping us work with our coaches to better understand how to translate the value of C-IQ into a humanizing language that the world can understand.

Other colleagues who add new dimensions to C-IQ are Sandra Foster, PhD, Debra Pearce McCall, PhD, and Marcia Ruben, PhD, who are working with us to expand our access to research focusing on the neuroscience of conversations. My husband Richard Glaser, PhD, brings his depth of knowledge to all of us, from the scientists to the practitioners, and to the executives who want to embrace the science as well as the practical wisdom. We are also partnering with the HeartMath Institute, headed by Deborah Rozman, PhD, and with whom we will be doing intensive research on how HeartMath and Conversational Intelligence can supply more insights about the neuroscience of conversations.

Moving forward, we are expanding across all businesses, from the small to the large, as well as expanding into specific uses for Conversational Intelligence, such as C-IQ for Sales, C-IQ for Educators, and in the future even C-IQ for Couples.

I am more and more convinced every day by our research and by the influx of interest in C-IQ that through our conversations we connect and communicate and drive the growth in our brains and in our lives. Conversations are the source of energy that moves us out of our doldrums when we are sad, and are the power that launches transformational products into the world. Conversations are the golden threads that enable us to move toward, and trust others, but these threads can also unravel, causing us to run from others in fear of loss and pain.

Words are not things—they are the representations and symbols we use to view, think about, and process our perceptions of reality, and they are our means of sharing these perceptions with others. Yet until the vocabulary of neuroscience filtered into our everyday lexicon, few leaders were able to understand how vital conversations are to the health and productivity of their company's culture.

Unhealthy conversations are at the root of distrust, deceit, betrayal, and avoidance—which leads to lower productivity, lower innovation, and ultimately, lower success. By understanding how conversations trigger different parts of our brain, and how they either catalyze or "freeze" our brains in protective patterns, you can develop the conversational skills that propel individuals, teams, and organizations toward success. *Conversational Intelligence is both instinctual and learnable,* and it is necessary to build healthier, more resilient organizations in the face of change.

A seemingly simple act such as talking with a colleague—a short exchange of words in a hallway—has the ability to alter someone's life permanently. Phrases like *"You can't do that!"* and *"If you only knew how!"* may take only seconds to utter, but they can be life changing. There is little connection between the time it takes to say the words and the last-ing impact they may have on a person, a relationship, or an organization. Because our words are so powerful, we must understand and develop Conversational Intelligence, a framework and perspective that lets us see how conversations create powerful links between relationships and cul-ture. Conversations are the way we connect, engage, navigate, and trans-form the world with others.

The premise of Conversational Intelligence is: *"To get to the next level of greatness depends on the quality of our culture, which depends on the quality of our rela-tionships, which depends on the quality of our conversations. Everything happens through conversations!"*[4]

I. **Conversational Intelligence gives us the power to influence our neu-rochemistry, even in the moment.** Every conversation we have with another person has a chemical component. Conversations have the power to change the brain—they stimulate the production of hor-mones and neurotransmitters, stimulate body systems and nerve pathways, and change our body's chemistry, not just for a moment but perhaps for a lifetime.

At the simplest level, we say something and we get a response—I ask you a question and you tell me the answer. However, conversations can quickly become more complex as questions provoke thoughts and feel-ings about what you mean or your intentions, and this stirs our chemi-cal networks into action. If questions feel threatening, we do more than answer; we activate networks inside the brain to "handle" the threat.

2. **Conversational Intelligence gives us the power to express our inner thoughts and feelings to one another in ways that can strengthen relationships and success.** As we communicate, we read the content and emotions being sent our way and we likewise send content and emotions to others. Conversations are more than the information we

share and the words we speak. They offer a way to package our feelings about our world, others, and ourselves. As leaders, we communicate that we are *sad* or *happy* with almost every conversation. As we come to understand the power of language in regulating how people feel every day, and the role language plays in the brain's capacity to expand perspectives and create a "feel good" experience, we can learn to shape our workplace in profound ways.

3. **Conversational Intelligence gives us the power to influence the way we interpret reality.** Conversations impact different parts of the brain in different ways, because different parts of the brain are listening for different things. By understanding the way conversations impact our listening we can determine how we listen—and how we listen determines how we interpret and make sense of our world.

Epigenetics of Conversations

Some of the most exciting new research coming from the field of epigenetics is emerging to validate the importance and power of conversations in shaping our DNA. What we are learning is that all of genes are not equal. There are genes—called *template genes*—that give us a foundation of stable and unchangeable characteristics.

Even more recently, scientists have identified what are called *transcription genes,* which are encoded to be impacted by the environment. They are genes that can be influenced; they are changeable.

Scientists are validating the power and importance of the quality of our conversations. Through conversations we can turn genes on and off. Why is this so important for us to know? In simple terms, our template genes are those that are not changeable, while transcription genes are specifically designed to be impacted by the interactions we have with others. Conversations influence us more than we ever imagined! And "conversations" and our conversational influence doesn't stop when we become adults, it continues throughout our lifetime!

Conversational Intelligence gives us a new way to look at the power of our interactions with others. It gives us a new and innovative framework for exploring how conversations can influence culture, partnerships, teams, and relationships. How we influence each other through conversations is key to creating a healthy culture at work. Writing and developing Conversational Intelligence methodologies was my way of honoring the power of conversations in shaping our environment for success, and also for influencing our DNA. Our transcription genes are designed "for influence" and our body of work supported by the new insights coming from the field of epigenetics and neuroscience is giving us new insights and guidance for diving even deeper into the field of Conversational Intelligence.

INC. magazine identified Conversational Intelligence as one of the top five business trends in 2016,[5] and Microsoft has said that Conversational Intelligence is spawning new innovations and influencing their product development for the next decade.[6]

What Is Conversational Intelligence?

In working with hundreds of companies and tens of thousands of employees in many of the nation's largest organizations over the last thirty years, I've discovered that a lack of Conversational Intelligence is at the root of breakdowns in many relationships. Simply put, Conversational Intelligence is essential to an organization's ability to create shared meaning about what needs to be accomplished and why, so that employees get excited and are clear about the future they are helping to create together.

Conversational Intelligence will enable you to discern the types of conversations that are suited for different situations. At one end of the conversational continuum are conversations that allow us to transact business and share information with one another, which I call Level I. As we move across the continuum we engage in "positional" conversations—those in which we have a strong voice and point of view, and work to influence others to understand or accept our view of the world; these are Level II conversations. And as we reach the highest level, which I call Level III, we are communicating with others to transform and together shape reality, and I refer to this powerful type of conversations Co-creating Conversations®. Co-creating Conversations are the highest form of conversation; they not only let us advance our conversations with others, I believe they are actually writing new "DNA" that can be passed along to the next generation. Co-creation is a set of skills and a complementary mind-set that enable you to have extraordinary, transformational conversations with others.

Do we all have the ability to reach Level III? Researchers in neuroscience are demonstrating that the capacity to operate at Level III is hardwired into all human beings, present in our more recently developed brain, the prefrontal cortex (or executive brain). Our prefrontal cortex is activated when we feel we can trust others, and is deactivated when we feel high levels of fear and distrust. All human beings are "built for Level III" yet most environments do not encourage this capacity in us, and many in fact discourage it. Understanding all three levels of Conversational Intelligence and how to activate them is vital to success.

As a starting place, it's important to know that Conversational Intelligence is a competence that can be cultivated. It allows us to connect, engage, and navigate with others, and it is the single most important intelligence that gets better when "we" do it, meaning that our individual capacity for Conversational Intelligence expands when we practice it with others and when we all focus on it together. While the other intelligences are more "I-centric" in nature—they are intelligences we develop individually, such as mathematical intelligence or linguistic intelligence—Conversational Intelligence exists as a collaborative effort, and when we practice it together we raise the C-IQ of relationships, and we can also raise the C-IQ of teams and organizations.

And, because C-IQ leverages all other kinds of individual intelligences, there is neither a more powerful skill nor a more necessary one to master.

Conversational Intelligence provides a framework and practices for the way individuals, teams, and organizations listen, engage, architect, and influence the moment and shape the future, in all situations. When we use our C-IQ in business we strengthen the organization's culture in order to achieve greater business results. Understanding how to "level set" our conversations gives us the power to transform reality.

The Map Is Not the Territory

In 1931, Alfred Korzybski, a Polish-American scientist and philosopher, coined the phrase "the map is not the territory" to distinguish the words we use to describe reality from reality itself. Korzybski said that we often confuse the map (the way our minds represent reality) with the territory (our physical reality) and don't realize we are confusing the two. We communicate with others as though we all share the same map—and the same world—which causes conflict and collisions.

To become good at C-IQ, we need to recognize that "the map is not the territory" and spend more time joining the two through conversations. What makes C-IQ so exciting as a discipline is that, through the incredible amount of neuroscience research taking place around the world right now, we are able to understand more about the way our mind creates biases, blind spots, and filters that prevent us from seeing reality as it is. Understanding the science behind conversations will appear throughout the book. As importantly, we are learning from coaches, consultants, and people who are learning to boost their Conversational Intelligence that this knowledge plus the related skills are not only learnable, they are essential for our success as individuals, teams, and organizations—even as a species. Conversational Intelligence is about creating an ongoing dialogue with others, to explore our maps, which I refer to as our "movies"—and to stay in touch with one another's evolution of thinking as we work together to achieve shared goals. Whether you are working in a small business or a large global company, elevating your C-IQ will be a lifechanging experience that will not only yield business results, it will create new energy for transformation and growth.

Turning Adversaries into Partners

My earliest official foray into teaching people about Conversational Intelligence began with one of my first clients, Boehringer Ingelheim, a global pharmaceutical company that hired me to work with its sales training and development group. When we started the project, BI sales representatives were not getting as many appointments with doctors—who make decisions about what drugs to prescribe—as were reps from other pharmaceutical companies, which translated directly into fewer sales and lower profits. In a comparison of the sales forces of forty pharmaceutical companies, Boehringer was rated thirty-ninth, not exactly a great position. My job was to figure out what Boehringer's sales reps were doing to create so much resistance, and then to design a program to help the BI Sales Development team build rapport with doctors.

Over a period of weeks, the BI team and I plunged into our discovery work. We observed dozens of typical sales calls—with new reps as well as seasoned ones—and then we deconstructed the sales encounter, mapping the conversations and their outcomes. We paid special attention to nonverbal cues, including tone of voice and body language like posture and facial expression.

The BI sales reps had been taught to use a traditional features-and-benefits model of selling. This meant that if the physician raised concerns about the product during a sales call, reps were taught to "handle objections" by either providing additional facts about the product or by trying to persuade the physician that her issue was not really important.

This approach was based on using rational arguments and supporting data to "make the objections go away."

Even the word "objections" assumes an adversarial relationship, though the reps didn't realize that—they had been taught to handle them, and handle them they did. Because they saw their success as dependent upon eliminating objections, they became very good at argument and persuasive language. However, the physicians on the other end of the conversations sensed that they were being steamrolled, which led them to stiffen their resistance or try to end the appointment as soon as possible. Rather than connecting with the sales reps, the doctors we observed showed nonverbal signs of pushing them away.

Change One Thing, Change Everything

The doctors that Boehringer sales reps called on quickly learned to see the reps as adversaries rather than friends. Not only did the moments of contact make no progress toward "Getting to WE," the meetings became power struggles during which the sales reps unintentionally encouraged the doctors to write them off instead of writing their prescriptions.

Eureka! Now that we had discovered the problem, we decided that instead of focusing on "handling objections," the reps should eliminate that phrase from their vocabulary altogether. We taught them how to reframe the interaction and use a new word to label what was going on. We asked reps to consider their interactions with the physician from a new point of view—to pay close attention to nonverbal cues and to be more sensitive to the impact they were having. During this process we helped the reps completely reframe their view of the physicians' questions; where they once saw questions as objections, they now were encouraged to see them as simple requests for additional information. This new way of viewing the sales dynamic had a profound effect on the relationship between sales rep and physician, resulting in a shift away from handling physician objections and toward building a relationship with the physician. What happens *at the moment of contact* defines the relationship. As the reps learned how to shift from focusing on selling first (and often it was hard selling) to *"relationship before task,"* the physicians felt that the reps and BI as a company were partnering with them in helping better serve their patients. At a deeper level, the physicians began to trust their BI reps, and BI's business increased.

Within a year, both peers and customers ranked the Boehringer Ingelheim sales force as one of the most respected sales organizations in the pharmaceutical business. We gave the program the acronym "BEST," which stood for Boehringer Ingelheim Effective Sales Training, and it enabled the sales executives to become the best in the industry.

The Neuroscience of WE

What we learned from deconstructing the moment of contact in the sales calls between the physicians and the reps supports what I call the *Neuroscience of WE*. During their early interactions, the sales reps were triggering the physicians' amygdala, a part of the brain that has long been associated with our mental and emotional fear state. By turning their meetings with doctors into a battle, the sales reps were activating the circuitry of fight and flight rather than creating in the doctors a desire to prescribe Boehringer products. Without realizing it, the physicians were reacting instinctively. They were closing down and protecting themselves from potential harm.

To get to the root of the issue, I developed a program that taught the sales reps STAR Skills™—Skills That Achieve Results. Those skills are: (1) building rapport; (2) listening without judgment; (3) asking discovery questions; (4) reinforcing success; and (5) dramatizing the message. These skills are simple, powerful, and get at the heart of building trusting relationships. They draw on a part of the brain known as the

STAR SKILLS™

FIGURE I–1: Star Skills

reticular activating system (RAS), associated with many vitally important functions. The most critical component of selling is conscious and focused attention.

Building rapport focuses us on getting on the same wavelength as the person with whom we are talking. Listening without judgment involves paying full attention to the other person as he speaks, while consciously setting aside the tendency to judge the other person. Asking discovery question opens our minds to the power of curiosity, as well as to the possibility of changing our views as we listen and learn. Reinforcing success and dramatizing the message, the last two skills, also play a role in sustaining a healthy trusting relationship. Reinforcing success focuses us on seeing and validating what "success looks like" for both people—which eliminates uncertainty and moves people into action through greater connectivity and coherence. Dramatizing the message is a reminder that we need to be alert to whether our messages are clear and understood by others. When we fail to connect in the way we communicate, we can try saying it another way—telling a story or showing a picture of what we're trying to say. These dramatizations move us toward greater understanding with others, elevating trust and strengthening the relationship. This elevates our awareness to stay in sync until we are certain we are on the same wavelength. When we are, we achieve coherence with others. STAR skills serve as guideposts for our engagement process, but they are also designed to create a positive shift in brain chemistry. Supportive engagement makes us feel safe, as the oxytocin we release during such conversations enhances our feelings of bonding, and dopamine and serotonin contribute to feelings of well-being. These neurotransmitters tamp down the defensive role of the amygdala, freeing the prefrontal cortex—the more recently evolved part of the human brain—to allow new ideas, insights, and wisdom to emerge. This part of the brain also contains the mirror neurons that allow us to feel empathy for one another.

When I was working with Boehringer, scientists were not yet using fMRIs (functional magnetic resonance imaging) to look inside our brains at the moment of social contact. No one could actually see inside the minds of the sales reps and doctors to see when they were in sync, yet we could certainly observe what happened when they *did* learn to build trust. The sales reps' use of the five STAR skills had an extraordinary impact on the physicians, quelling the doctors' more primal reactions and allowing the reps to engage the more positive impulses that some researchers call the "heart brain." Using STAR skills, the reps were also able to engage the doctors' prefrontal cortex, with its ability for strategy and planning. We know strategies worked because not only did this shift lead to more open communication and higher levels of trust during sales calls, it led to higher levels of commitment to the Boehringer brand and its products.

Through the STAR skills program, the reps learned to not only change their language but to create a totally new relationship with physicians, moving from adversaries to trusted partners. Within eighteen months, Boehringer Ingelheim had dramatically increased sales and expanded its market share. In industry comparisons, BI's sales reps moved from number thirty-nine to number one in the eyes of physicians. What started with a simple process of deconstructing the conversations between reps and doctors ended with an incredible success story that has continued for more than twenty years. As reps and physicians embraced the new approach, profits soared.

Success is contagious, and our work had a ripple effect across the company. Soon, management and leadership teams wanted to adopt the collaborative approach we had created with their sales reps, so we continued to build leadership, innovation, and management programs all across BI. Today, more than two decades later, the sales team is still using this approach as the foundation of their sales training programs and for advanced sales development programs for seasoned reps.

Creating the Conversational Space for Mindfulness

Conversations have purpose in our lives. The most exciting work you'll learn about in this book is how to navigate the three levels of conversations: Level I—transactional (how to exchange data and information); Level II—positional (how to work with power and influence); and Level III—transformational (how to co-create the future for mutual success). All three levels are hardwired into our brains, and all are important. We can get stuck in any one of them and find that our conversations become unhealthy and lead to distrust, or we can thrive in all of them and find that our conversations are not only healthy but achieve transformational results. Healthy conversations are built on high levels of trust, and throughout *Conversational Intelligence* you will learn more about the three levels of conversation.

According to the research of Angelika Dimoka, PhD, and other neuroscientists who use fMRI (functional magnetic resonance imaging) technology to study what happens inside the brain, trust is centered in the prefrontal cortex and distrust in the amygdala and limbic areas of the brain. How do we know? These areas light up when a research subject is asked to respond to questions or to perform activities that stimulate "trust" or "distrust." The networks involving trust and distrust are, of course, complex, however it's important to know that their locations in the brain are distinct—the fact that the brain processes these two responses separately offers a core insight into how to develop Conversational Intelligence. We can't connect to others if our amygdala is overactive. Fear and distrust close down our brains.

This book focuses on how you can create the conversational space that creates *deeper understanding* and *engagement* rather than *fear* and *avoidance*.

As you read and absorb the wisdom garnered from my thirty years of client engagements, I will ask you right up front to "prime your pump" as you read, and to remember these three things:

I. **Be mindful of your conversations and the emotional content you bring—either pain or pleasure.** Are you sending friend or foe messages? Are you sending the message *"You can trust me to have your best interest at heart"* or *"I want to persuade you to think about things my way?"*

When you're aware of these meta-messages, you can create a safe culture that allows all parties to interact at the highest level, sharing perspectives, feelings, and aspirations and elevating *insights* and *wisdom*.

2. **Conversations have the ability to trigger emotional reactions.** Conversations carry meaning—and meaning is embedded in the listener even more than in the speaker. Words either cause us to bond and trust more fully, thinking of others as friends and colleagues, or they cause us to break rapport and think of others as enemies. Your mind will open as you see the connection between language and health, and you'll learn how to create healthy organizations through your conversational rituals.

3. **Remember, the words we use in our conversations are rarely neutral.** Words have *histories* informed by years of use. Each time a new experience overlays another meaning on a word, the information all gets collected in our brains to be activated *during conversations*. Knowing how you project meaning into your conversations will enable you to connect with others and, in so doing, let go of much of the self-talk that diverts you from working together effectively.

By understanding how conversations trigger different parts of the brain and stimulate certain habits and behaviors, you can develop and grow your Conversational Intelligence to build healthier, more resilient organizations in the face of change.

Enjoy the ride!

PART I

Conversational Intelligence and Why We Need It

1

What We Can Learn from
Our Worst Conversations!

*I know that you believe you understand what you think I said, but I'm not
sure you realize that what you heard is not what I meant.*

—PENTAGON SPOKESMAN ROBERT MCCLOSKEY
DURING A PRESS BRIEFING ABOUT THE VIETNAM WAR

Conversations are multidimensional, not linear. What we *think*, what
we *say*, what we *mean*, what others *hear*, and *how we feel about it afterward*
are the key dimensions behind Conversational Intelligence. Though
conversations are not simply "ask and tell" levels of discourse, we often
treat them as though they are.

Good Intentions, Bad Impact

A decade ago, I had a coaching client who I knew from the outset was
going to be challenging. As it turned out, we fired each other after six
months. None of us likes to fail, let alone anticipate the prospect of
failure. When my client—let's call him Anthony—interacted with me,
he came across as a tough, arrogant executive who lived inside his head
and didn't share his feelings. In retrospect, I know we were caught in

our biases about each other and about what coaching involved. I was trapped in a dance of distrust with my client, but at the time, I didn't know enough to understand that I, the coach, was being thrown off by the very set of skills I would acquire over the next fifteen years.

Coaching requires that you know yourself first; from that platform you can help others know themselves. If a coach—in this case, me—is not seasoned enough or aware enough to handle a difficult client like Anthony, she is not the right coach. But I didn't know this yet, and I plowed forward in our conversations, believing I would figure out a way to penetrate his shell and connect with him.

Feel-Good and Feel-Bad Conversations

When we are having a good conversation, even if it's a difficult one, we feel good. We feel connected to the other person in a deep way and we feel we can trust him. *In good conversations, we know where we stand with others—we feel safe.*

In our research over thirty years, trust is brought up as a key descriptor of a good conversation. People will say, "I feel open and trusting. I could say what was on my mind." Or, "I don't have to edit anything, and I can trust it won't come back to hurt me."

Conversations are the golden threads, albeit sometimes fragile ones, that keep us connected to others. And why is that important? Human beings have hardwired systems exquisitely designed to let us know where we stand with others; based on our quick read of a situation, our brains know whether we should operate in a protective mode or be open to sharing, discovery, and influence.

The neural network that allows us to connect with other human beings was discovered in 1926 by Constantin von Economo, who came across unusually shaped long neurons in two places—in the prefrontal cortex of the brain—the anterior cingulate cortex (ACC) and in the fronto-insular (FI) cortex. What von Economo discovered is that these neurons extend into the gut, literally the stomach, and inform our instinctive network by responding to socially relevant cues—be it a frowning face, a grimace of pain, or simply the voice of someone we love.[1] This network of special neurons, now referred to as VENs, enables us to keep track of social cues and allows us to alter our behavior accordingly.[2] This is one of our most powerful and profoundly active networks, yet it is one relatively rarely discussed in the neuroscience literature. My assumption is that it's not discussed because researchers are still not sure how it impacts observable behavior, which is easier to study than instincts or intuition. Networks connected with the stomach—often referred to as "gut instinct"—are simply a difficult research subject. It is much harder to design a study and draw conclusions about internal workings than about behavior—and scientific research is designed to help us draw conclusions. When we are in conversation with others, perhaps even before we open our mouths, we size them up and determine whether we trust or distrust them; once this happens, our brains are ready to either open up or close down. Bad conversations trigger our distrust network and good conversations trigger our trust network. Each influences what we say, how we say it, and why we say it, and the networks even have a heavy hand in shaping the outcomes of each conversation.

Conversations Trigger Neurochemistry

At the moment we make contact with other people, biochemical reactions are triggered at every level of our bodies. Our heart responds in two ways—electrochemical and chemical. When we interact with others we have a biochemical or neurochemical response to the interaction, and we pick up electrical signals from others as well. As our bodies read a person's energy—which we pick up within ten feet of the person—the process of connectivity begins. We experience others through electrical energy, feelings, which we have at the moment of contact; on top of this we layer our old memories about the person, ideas, beliefs, or stuff we make up, all while trying to make sense of who he is. Can we trust him? Will he hurt us? Can we connect and add value to each other's lives?

Making Stuff Up

What made my conversations with my former client Anthony so bad? Many of us have grown up believing that conversations occur when two people give and receive information from each other. What we know today is that conversations are multidimensional and multi-temporal. That means that some parts of the brain process information more quickly than others, and our feelings emerge before we are able to put words to them. The things we *say*, the things we *hear*, the things we *mean*, and the way we *feel* after we say it may all be separate, emerging at different times; so you can see how conversations are not just about sharing information—they are part of a more complex conversational equation. When what we say, what we hear, and what we mean are not in agreement, we retreat into our heads and make up stories that help us reconcile the discrepancies.

My frustration with not being able to have an open and trusting conversation with Anthony led me to start making "movies" about him in my head while we conversed. I found myself being very critical of Anthony's ways, his style of talking and his intentions. I found myself leaving empathy behind and putting judgment first. I imagined Anthony as an arrogant bully and continued to embellish my feelings about him until I cast him as the worst leader I had ever met. At times, I imagined that Anthony didn't *have* any feelings, and was out to prove that he was right and I was wrong. The better my moviemaking abilities got, the less able I was to really connect with him and help him as a coach.

To be fair, Anthony had a huge challenge in front of him. He had been hired as the new president of a global publishing company poised to transform its offerings from print to digital. Some saw Anthony as the next CEO, conditional upon his successful completion of my six-month executive coaching process. We both had a lot riding on our engagement.

Failure to Connect

I'm not sure if it was my fear of failure or Anthony's stubbornness and low level of awareness that took me off my game or—worse yet—a combination of both. I was convinced that he didn't get how important *connecting* was, and I also told myself he didn't really care. By the time I had cast our relationship in hopeless terms, I was unable to do what a good coach should do: facilitate a wake-up call for change. Instead, by slipping into my own moviemaking, I contributed to our failure to connect.

After making several attempts to put the subject of connectivity on the table with Anthony during our first few coaching sessions, I realized that he, too, was composing, directing, and starring in a "movie in his mind" about who he was, what he needed to do to be successful, and why I was wrong and he was right. I remember leaving one of the early sessions feeling insecure about my coaching abilities. At times, I even felt like the coaching roles had changed: he was driving and I was being taken along for the ride. In my mind, I had really messed up as Anthony's coach. I failed to connect on the very important subject of connecting, and this missed opportunity could be life changing for him—and perhaps even life changing for me.

The Push and Pull of Conversations

Upon reflection, I realize my fear of failure made me push Anthony harder. We were both caught up in being right and neither of us knew it. When we are trapped in our need to be right, we want to win, we fight to win, and we go into overdrive trying to persuade others to our point of view.

When we are out to win at all costs, we operate out of the part of the limbic brain called the amygdala. This part is hardwired along with

OUR PRIMITIVE AND EXECUTIVE BRAINS

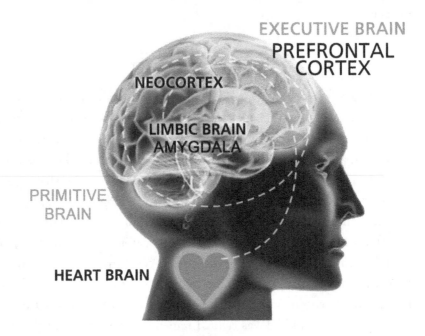

FIGURE 1–1: Our Primitive and Executive Brains

the well-developed instincts of fight, flight, freeze, or appease, located in the primitive brain, that have evolved over millions of years. When we feel threatened, the amygdala activates the immediate impulses that ensure we survive. Our brains lock down and we are no longer open to influence.

On the other side of the brain spectrum is the prefrontal cortex. This is the newest brain, and it enables us to build societies, have good judgment, be strategic, handle difficult conversations, and build and sustain trust. Yet when the amygdala picks up a threat, our conversations are subject to the lockdown, and we get more "stuck" in our point of view!

"You've got to be nicer to people," I found myself saying to Anthony, as though telling or yelling would make him think in new ways. I was falling into the traps I teach leaders not to fall into—I was triggered, I was biased, and I couldn't recover in the moment. Recovery, one of the skills I so dutifully teach others to use—was out of my grasp at the moment I needed it most. (More about pattern interrupt, refocusing reframing, and redirecting in chapter 8, "Conversational Agility.")

"Nice is not important," Anthony said; now trying to convince me that his view of reality was more real than mine. "My job is getting the next strategy in place and I've got to focus on who on my team can be a producer, not who is nice. If I need to fire the top people on my staff, so be it. They're from the old school. They don't get the digital world and I don't need them here."

I was caught in the "Tell–Sell–Yell Syndrome": tell them once, try to sell them on the reason you are right, then yell! When we are in this posture, we are seeking to gain power over others, and I didn't realize the implications. Anthony was not listening. He didn't appear like he cared to. He was right, and others were wrong.

He showed little respect for all the years of learning and experience his team brought to the table, and I saw him as someone with his mind made up. He was forceful and single-minded in his efforts at persuasion, telling me why cleaning house was clearly the right strategy for success. While all my good instincts told me to help him explore the best way of getting to know his new company and culture during his first one hundred days, I was finding that task outside my skill set.

It's All in Your Head!

In different ways, I tried to initiate with Anthony the missing conversation about building trusting relationships and getting to know his team's real talents before taking drastic action. But the words didn't come out of my mouth in a way he could hear: I told him, "You must realize how important your feelings toward your people are in getting them to be good producers." I tried being eloquent and provocative—even straightforward—but I was not getting through.

I tried again: "You haven't even conversed openly with your team and found out what they can or cannot do. This is all in your head." In retrospect, I realize that the more I pushed the less he listened. His mind was closed to new ways of looking at the situation—he was emotional toward me and emotional about his prospects for success. "Right now, nothing is as important as the bottom line," Anthony said. "And that is what I've been chartered to do. Improve it!"

I could see the conversation was going nowhere, so I backed down and closed up. I was not being a good coach, much less a great one. I was hooked and triggered, all the things I had been trained not to do. Had I been smarter about connectivity back then, I would have known what to do to change the conversation with my client, and to bring him to a place of mindful awareness of the impact he was having on his team and on me. Instead, that day I became another casualty. (In part 2 you'll learn more about building your Third Eye skills for linking intention and impact.)

Reality Gaps

Anthony and I never built trust—the foundation for open, candid, caring conversations. Instead, I started to doubt myself and to distrust my instincts.

At that moment I had to consider: Could I step forward into a new place of trust with my client and speak the truth? Could I ask him to speak up and ask the important questions? Could I be so bold as to ask if we were right for each other as coach and coachee? Could I ask him if he was ready to look himself in the mirror from another's perspective?

Instead I reacted with fear. I was threatened. I was caught in my primitive brain. When we are in conversations and we experience gaps between what we feel in the moment, what we think, and what we mean, *then what we "hear" is altered toward distrust.*

Meaning

Most people assume that meaning is embedded in the words they speak. But according to forensic linguists, meaning is far more vaporous, teased into existence through vocalized puffs of air, hand gestures, body tilts, dancing eyebrows, and nuanced nostril flares. The transmission of meaning still involves primate mechanics worked out during the Pliocene epoch. And context is crucial; when we try to record a conversation, we are capturing only part of the gestalt of that moment. What might appear to be a solid audio recording can easily morph into an acoustic Rorschach test.[3]

In the moment, I was caught in a dozen strong and confusing feelings that clogged our conversations and caused me more fear. Unable to put words to how I was feeling, I went inside my own mind and made more movies. These movies were about how wrong he was, about how closed he was, about how unable I was to move him forward and therefore perhaps not a good coach after all.

Anthony and I fired each other soon after that, and, as it turned out, within six months he was asked to leave the company. While he failed to connect with his organization in ways that would help him work out the challenges the company was facing, I failed to help him open up his mind so that he might begin to see the world through others' eyes.

Distrust Is the Road to Nowhere

No matter what we're doing in our professional lives, trust is the single most important element in the process I call "Creating WE," which, in my many years of working as a consultant and executive coach, I have found to be the best way of achieving extraordinary, sustainable success in business and in life. WE (and what I sometimes call WE-centric Leadership) is built on a level of trust that binds us together. When it dissolves, like it did with my client Anthony, so does our ability to treat one another with empathy and understanding, and to work together to create a business enterprise that is bigger than the sum of its parts.

Before we can interact openly with others we need to answer this question: Are you a friend or an enemy? This profound question is hard-wired in us—it's been honed by evolution, and our lives have depended on answering the question correctly for millions of years. Our brains have evolved to make that decision so quickly that we might not even know it has taken place. After all, we couldn't make our contribution to the gene pool if we had to spend a lot of our time thinking about whether or not to run from that saber-toothed tiger that just stepped out of the jungle.

Today, in business, our literal survival may not depend on toggling between friend or foe decisions from moment to moment, but our brains don't know that. To us, our livelihood may feel like a life-or-death issue. Having our ideas attacked in a meeting or being dressed down by the boss still triggers our brain's fight–flight–freeze response, and can drive us to react in ways that seriously undermine our best interests.

How important is understanding what happens at the moment of contact to you? I believe it's essential to your future and to the success of the company you work for. Its effect can be felt right at the first moment of contact and continues through the life of a relationship. That first greeting, handshake, telephone call, or e-mail sets the stage for a connection that could die in the first few seconds or lead to a lifetime of mutual support and prosperity. If we don't get past that first moment of contact in our conversations with others, we will revisit our decision to trust the other person not just once but many, many times, so the issue of trust will continue to be of paramount importance.

Consider the metaphor of a door that guards the pathway to our inner self. When we feel trust, we readily open that door, leading to an exchange of thoughts, feelings, and dreams with someone else. When we distrust someone, on the other hand, thinking that she is somehow a threat, we quickly slam that door shut in an effort to defend ourselves from being hurt or rejected. Unfortunately, our brains don't always make the best judgments relative to our long-term interests. It's all too likely we are misinterpreting the signals we're receiving from our bosses, coworkers, and employees, especially in a workplace with high levels of stress and an abundance of deadline pressure.

Over the course of my career, I have become deeply immersed in the neuroscience of WE to better understand how people impact one another, both in times of stress and in times of health. In all my research, I continue to return to "the moment of contact"—when we are in conversation with others. At this moment, the *quality* of the conversation drives the nature of the impact. At the moment of contact, conversations have the power to transform our lives. If the impact "feels good" we will open up to more interactions and grow. If the impact "feels bad" we will close down and move into protective mode. The chapters ahead will talk more about the power of conversations to trigger protection or growth.

How Conversations Shape Our Brains

My conversation with Anthony had a huge impact on me. It took more than a decade from that point in my work with Anthony for me to take another big leap forward into the anatomy of conversations. I discovered that by looking back at a conversation and deconstructing it, I was able to see what I was doing to impact the situation, either negatively or positively. I called this skill "looking back to look forward," and I found that it was a skill I could teach people. I also coined the term "deconstructing conversations" to mean examining conversations after the fact to garner new insights about them. My book-writing projects, *Creating WE* and *The DNA of Leadership*, were opportunities to put these new conversational skills to a test, to see if I could teach others conversational intelligence skills.

What I was discovering was wisdom relevant to all human beings. There were patterns about human interactions that we all shared, patterns that had to do with how conversations make us *healthy* or *unhealthy*. I was learning that, to be healthy, human beings need to connect, belong, and be strong. They must learn to have strong points of view, have a voice, *and* to partner with others. To sustain a feeling of safety (which our brains need for us to feel healthy), we've evolved instincts to protect ourselves or reject those who harm us. Yet if we manage our underlying feelings of rejection and protection, and we harness our ability to reach out to others—even when we are feeling rejected—we gain mastery over our instincts.

When we choose an action that moves us toward connecting with others, we physically excite different sets of neurons and ignite new ways of thinking that enable us to resist impulses from our primitive brain and instead access our executive brain. This huge insight was inspiring to my work.

I began to realize that the moment we enter into a conversation, our brains map our "interaction patterns," and we read a great deal of information from the dynamics of the interaction. We know if the person is a "giver, taker, or matcher."[4] We know whether the person is fair, honors our territory, will reciprocate, will collaborate, and will give us a chance to voice our thoughts. We know whether the person takes over the conversational space, or if she will share it. We know if we will be safe, if the person is friendly, or if she will harm us. We know whether we can trust him. All of this is hardwired into the way we process conversations, and I call this sensitivity we all have "vital instincts." They are the heartbeat behind our conversations.

Conversations are the social rituals that hold us together, the fabric of culture and society. Sometimes when we—as leaders—are marching forward, furiously achieving our goals and objectives, we fail to see the impact of these minute yet powerful interactions in conversations on others. Yet once we do, we can change the interaction dynamics and change our future forever!

Addicted to Being Right

When I got a call to interview for an executive coaching assignment at Verizon, I didn't have much hope. I learned the executive, Rob, had interviewed twelve executive coaches before me, and I was already doubting that I had a chance. I learned that, while the coaches were all good, none lived up to this executive's expectations. I learned later that the reason I got the engagement was that during the interview, I didn't make him wrong.[5] Instead I was curious and nonjudgmental, and wanted to understand the world from his eyes, a skill that would become a key theme in my work and which provides the core wisdom in this book.

In gathering information that would help me understand my new Verizon leader, I learned an important story. Employee complaints had come to the HR Department, and several of the top complaints were from Rob's key direct reports, who vehemently requested HR switch them into different departments. One guy who had been with the company for twenty-five years ended up in the hospital with a heart attack that almost took his life. He told HR he was willing to give up his pension to report to a different boss.

Based on the background from HR and a few other sources, I knew this engagement was in my sweet spot. The focus for our work was going to be—though not limited to—conversations.

As part of my discovery process I interviewed people who interacted with Rob, so I could uncover what was creating such physical trauma and pain among his team, and how much of this pain had to do with conversations. I felt like Sherlock Holmes on a new assignment—something was going on that was causing a breakdown in people's immune systems, and I had to figure out what it was.

First, I wanted to get Rob's perspective about his leadership; our conversation went like this:

Me: Tell me about your leadership style. What is it all about?
Rob: I see myself as a best practice leader.
Me: Tell me how.
Rob: I really see my job as developing people to their best.
Me: And what does best look like?
Rob: I send my people home with things to read about leadership. I make sure they are being challenged to do more and better every day. I hold them to their word, and make sure they deliver what they said they would. When we are doing work for the CEO, I make sure we go over each draft, again and again, until it's right and perfect. When I'm on the road, I call in and go over everyone's to-do list to make sure they have delivered on my expectations. That's what best looks like.
Me: And are they reaching their best?
Rob: Most are not, so I keep motivating them and pushing them... Hmm, maybe it's time to fire them.

The Worst Conversations at Work

The more data I uncovered, the more I realized I was sitting on a time bomb. Rob had become a driven leader. Without realizing it, and in the pursuit of his goals, he had become incredibly self-centered—what I call an "I-centric" leader. He was the center of the universe and saw the world only from his perspective. He resisted seeing himself as anything but a great leader and judged his direct reports harshly; hardly aware of or sympathetic to the impact he was having on them. In other words, he had good intentions with bad impact. Learning to help leaders connect their intentions and their impact is core to Conversational Intelligence, and it's a skill we'll talk more about in future chapters.

Rob had failed to engage with his team in transformational and meaningful ways. His conversations were all one way (telling people what to do), and he rarely listened to or noticed signs of life in others. He had fallen into the most vicious trap any leader can get caught in, the Tell–Sell–Yell Syndrome we talked about earlier. The chief symptom of this malady is that the executive thinks that telling others what to do and how to do it is the essence of good leadership. Rob was stuck in a dynamic of "telling and selling" people on what he thought.

Rob failed to see the world from a WE-centric perspective. He didn't realize that his description of good leadership was all about him—about his expectations for others. In the pursuit of getting to the best, he didn't realize he was broadcasting messages of failure and disappointment with every interaction. His conversational patterns—his interaction dynamics—were "holding his team to the fire," and they burned.

Rob's team was so afraid of him that they, at first, refused to take part in the coaching process. They wanted out—or to have him fired. They wanted to move away so badly; imagine giving up a twenty-five-year pension just to stop the pain.

When I sat down with each direct report, one at a time, I learned what Rob was doing in great detail. One of the department's jobs was to create reports for the CEO about the financial markets and how the company's investments were doing. These were important reports, and if they weren't perfect, Rob and his team would look bad—so Rob thought. The direct reports referred to Rob's review process as "redlining." Each person would write a first draft and give it to Rob. Then he would correct it—redline it—and give it back. It would not have been so bad if there were only one or two iterations, but there were generally ten to fourteen revisions. One person said, "After a while, Rob was redlining his own writing, not ours. We are not valued, not treated with respect, diminished. We feel like kids back in elementary school with a horrible teacher redlining our work."

When I asked about the worst experiences Rob's direct reports had with him, each person recounted the same event: "Thanksgiving last year." "What happened?" I asked. "Rob set up a call with a client. He said it was necessary and we all had to attend. It was a virtual call with a financial institution that our company was doing business with. The company didn't honor Thanksgiving, so we had to be on the call. It was exactly when our families were having Thanksgiving dinner, and we missed being there. Not only did we miss it, we missed it for three hours. It was a long call and if we got off, all hell would have broken loose. We would have felt it for weeks afterwards."

My job was to coach Rob to see how his conversational patterns had created such stress and misery for everyone on his team—and how it had a ripple effect in the organization. His 360-feedback ratings had been the lowest among the team members for three years in a row.

When I asked his team, "What is one thing you would want Rob to change that would make a big difference in your life?" all reports focused on the same thing: their update calls and weekly meetings. His staff noted, "When Rob is traveling, we have phone calls to update us on our to-do lists. He never asks us how we're doing, he tells us what to do." The same was true for weekly meetings: "He goes around the table and asks about our progress—he treats us like children. It's insulting and embarrassing because if we are not in line with his expectations, he will say something about our progress and embarrass us in front of our colleagues. We live in a constant state of fear and stress."

When asked what one thing they would change beyond everything else, they replied, "Just for once, he should ask us what *we* think, or what *we* want to talk about, or what's on *our* minds."

Launching the Experiment

I finally made a breakthrough with Rob when I asked him to do an experiment and try just one new thing with his team. He agreed to change the way he ran his meetings. Rather than telling people what to do, he agreed to ask them for their ideas. It sounds like a simple request. For Rob, however, it was big one. Nonetheless, he managed to make the change and it had an incredibly powerful impact on his team. I got phone calls from everyone saying, "What did you give my boss to drink? He is a new person."

I asked what they meant by that, and each one said the same thing in different words: "I felt elated after our meeting. My whole body felt different. I didn't know what it felt like to be happy at work. He showed he cared about what we thought. His whole attitude toward us shifted from hating us to respecting us." "What did he do differently?" I asked. They told me, "He asked our opinions for the first time in four years."

Rob and I worked together to catalyze a transformation that changed his life and the lives of his staff. Once he experienced the power of this breakthrough and was able to shift from telling to asking, he was ready to leap into working on sharing and discovering—another powerful interaction dynamic that leads to building a collaborative workplace.

Rob continued to learn ways in which he made people feel motivated or demoralized at work, and put into place many new conversational rituals that changed the whole dynamic of his team and even their inter-actions with other departments. The next year Rob became the top-rated leader among the CEO's seven direct reports. He sustained that position year after year. He finally got it! He finally understood that conversations have a push and a pull, a feel-bad and feel-good compo-nent, and there are ingredients to great conversations that every leader should know.

In the next chapter we'll focus on conversations that can send us back into our primitive brain in a nanosecond: the conversations that cause us to get stuck in lower levels of engagement.

2

When We Lose Trust, We Lose Our Voice

You must trust and believe in people or life becomes impossible.

— ANTON CHEKHOV

I've been really fortunate to work with extraordinarily talented executives. They are smart, they are intuitive, and they are great leaders. They are men and women who are rising to the next levels in their careers—yet they have more to learn about how to lead. Ascending to the next level of leadership and leading thousands of people requires that they be able to think like an enterprise leader. This means having one eye on the future and the other on the present. Sometimes, that eye on the present "goes blind." While aspiring to the next level, we fail to see what is going on right in front of us.

How Good Intentions Go Bad

Kathryn was a star on the rise. With an Ivy League education and an impressive track record as a chief financial officer, Kathryn was on the short list of candidates to ascend to chief executive officer at her company, a global software provider. The problem was that, while no one doubted Kathryn's intellect—just about all of her peers used words like "brilliant" and "genius" to describe her—she was having trouble relating to employees who reported to her. It was the problems surrounding one employee in particular, a bright young woman named Margo, that led Kathryn to hire me as her coach.

Kathryn had worked with Margo for several years, during which time they successfully completed several high-profile projects that had drawn praise from the company's CEO and advisory board. But something had changed over a period of a few months. The most obvious symptom was that Margo's performance at work had fallen off dramatically, so much so that Kathryn was ready to demote or, worse, fire her. "We used to have such a great working relationship," Kathryn told me. "Now, I feel like Margo is only doing enough to get by. I can't afford to have someone working for me who I can't trust to get the job done." Before she made a decision about Margo's future, though, Kathryn asked me to talk to Margo to see if I could find out what had caused her performance to sour.

It didn't take me long to get to the root of the problem: the cooperative relationship these two intelligent and hard-working women once enjoyed had dissolved into distrust. While Margo couldn't pinpoint the exact moment things began to go downhill, she admitted that she had begun to look for ways to avoid working with Kathryn.

"Why?" I asked her. "Kathryn told me that not long ago the two of you had a great working relationship."

"I thought so, too," Margo responded. "But lately, it seems that she only criticizes me, or talks down to me when I don't come up with what she thinks are the 'right answers.' She acts as though she doesn't trust me anymore, and that hurts me."

"Can you give me an example?" I asked.

"Well, when we recently ran into an issue with one of our vendors, I tried to give Kathryn some suggestions about what we could do to solve the problem," Margo said. "That's when she snapped at me, saying things like, 'What do you mean by that?' or 'How can you even think that?' Kathryn is brilliant, but she has a hard time seeing things from someone else's point of view. And if you don't give her the answer she wants to hear, she stops trusting you to do your job. It's gotten so bad that I don't even bother bringing things up if I think Kathryn won't like them."

Reality Gaps

Does Margo's story sound familiar? Unfortunately, it's all too common for working relationships to sour over the issue of trust. In this case, Kathryn distrusted Margo to do her job the way Kathryn thought it should be done. As soon as Margo's approach seemed to veer off in different or new directions, Kathryn's behavior became testy and sometimes downright hostile. There was a reality gap, but neither knew it existed much less what to do about it.

Meanwhile, Margo had lost trust that Kathryn would appreciate her hard work and new ideas. The result, to put it bluntly, was that Margo's job was at risk over what I came to realize was a classic failure to exercise Conversational Intelligence. Both women were unable to deal with their fears and reestablish a trusting relationship. They might have known in their hearts that what would change everything was a dose of honest communication and direct feedback, but they could no quicker get there than a handcuffed person could get free. They didn't have the key!

Deconstructing Conversations

Kathryn and Margo's internal images of what "good" looked like had split apart through failure to check in with each other, to take the time to validate shared success, and to reaffirm their relationship. Instead, Margo's sensitivity to how her boss felt about her, and her fear and uncertainty about where she stood in Kathryn's eyes, caused her to begin creating her own interpretations of reality—"the movies of the mind." Rather than using her Conversational Intelligence to step into conversations about reality to restore trust, Margo felt afraid. And Kathryn, for her part, had done much the same thing.

23

How the Brain Responds to (Dis)Trust

As you are learning, we have distrust networks and trust networks. Once triggered, one becomes the master and the other the slave. They operate as a system; we can't turn either of them off, yet we can influence them.

With the ability to see inside the brain through fMRI (functional magnetic resonance imaging) scans and other sophisticated tools, scientists are able to identify the neural pathways that are activated when trust is either created or destroyed.

The Backstory on Trust and Distrust

Trust and distrust have different addresses in the brain. Trust is not just the absence of distrust; the two take place in different parts of the brain, according to Angelika Dimoka of the Center for Neural Decision Making at the Fox School of Business, Temple University. Distrust is signaled through the amygdala and trust is signaled through the prefrontal cortex. As we've seen, the prefrontal cortex is where we compare our expectations of what will happen (or what does happen) against reality. This is where we match our worldview with that of other people; where those views align we feel the greatest trust. This doesn't mean we can't disagree with others. In fact, we often put the greatest trust in those with whom we can disagree without negative consequences.

When employees are given honest feedback, even if the feedback suggests they have room to improve or change, the conversation can have a powerful impact, energizing them and motivating them to access new skills and talents. When handled well, honest feedback triggers growth, and employees will trust this feedback in the future. Yet when the interaction feels judgmental, unfair, or dishonest, an entirely different cascade of neurotransmitters creates a very different—and often distrustful—brain landscape for our future interactions.

What happens when we are uncertain? We've seen that trust and distrust take place in different parts of the brain, yet there is one place where trust and distrust overlap—and that is where we assess **uncertainty**.

While trust takes place in the prefrontal areas of the brain where we are assessing the credibility, intentions, and predictability of a person's behavior in the future, distrust takes place in the lower brain, where we are assessing another person's threat level, for this is the area of the brain where we experience the fear of loss. Researchers have linked the orbitofrontal cortex to uncertainty,[1] and demonstrated that activating this part of the brain increases distrust. At the moment of contact, when we engage with others and feel uncertainty about how to interpret the interaction, our orbitofrontal cortex activates.

Humans are designed to partner, and we do this on many complex levels. We form partnerships, we form teams, we form companies, and we form societies that depend on one another. To form partnerships as complex as those humans create, we need to have the neural circuitry to build trust. It appears that there is a neural circuit, called the insula (located below the prefrontal cortex), that acts as an information highway between our mirror neurons and the limbic system, thereby giving us the ability to broadcast messages throughout our brainstem. This may explain how we resonate or don't resonate with others—which is foundational to building trust. In the next chapter, we'll further explore how to increase our chances of building trust while also reducing feelings of uncertainty and distrust.

In Sync, Out of Sync

Conflicts that arise from opposing interpretations of reality, like we've seen in the case of Kathryn and Margo, are among the most common threats to trust. These conflicts trigger an array of fears about where we stand with other people. When people focus their attention on their fears, like loss of approval, as was the case with Margo, their minds fall victim to the neurochemistry of fear. Our fear-based neural networks are then activated, causing us to process reality though a fear-based lens instead of a trust-based one.

Being in sync with others is vital to healthy relationships. And it's not just a metaphor. Research indicates that when we are comfortable with someone, our heartbeat becomes more coherent, sending signals to the brain to relax, open up, and share with that person.[2] When gaps arise between what we expect and what we get, we become uncertain of our relationship and our fear networks begin to take control of our brains. As a result, we find ourselves lacking the neurochemical and hormonal support for placing trust in others. Our good judgment gives way to defensive, aggressive, or passive–aggressive behaviors that have a huge impact on our ability to be effective at our jobs. Our challenge, there-fore, is to find ways to head off our fears or, at the very least, understand where they may be coming from so we can work backward to find a solution. (We'll learn more about this in chapter 7, Priming for Level III Conversations.)

Amygdala Hijacking

Protecting ourselves is hardwired in our brains. The story of Kathryn and Margo helps illustrate what happens when the amygdala is hijacked, or triggered by the threat signals that shut the door to our higher brain centers. Think of phrases that we all use, such as, "I've never seen you act that way before" or, "This is not like you." Fear and conflict not only change the chemistry of the brain, they also change how we feel, how we behave, and how others perceive us. In a nanosecond we can move from being seen as a trusted friend and advisor to being seen as a frightening threat, a person deeply distrusted, because fear has tipped the scales that way.

Worse yet, when the amygdala goes into overdrive, it activates the limbic area of the brain, which stores all of our old memories. Once triggered, this part of the brain begins to remember other similar hurts and threats, and lumps them together into that movie I referred to earlier. Without our even realizing it, the moviemaking mind can take old memories and edit them into a new scary movie, giving our current

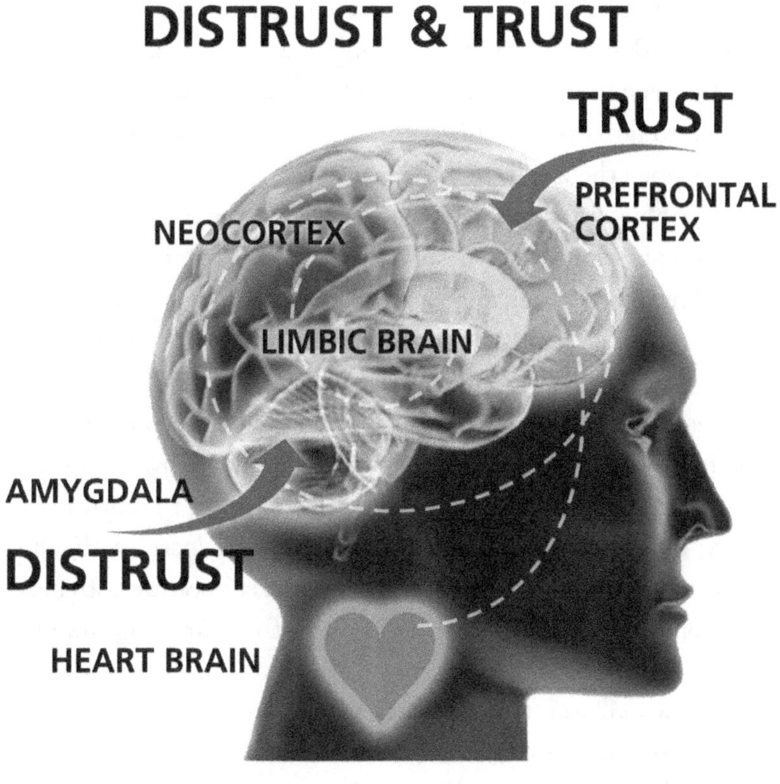

FIGURE 2–1: Distrust and Trust

situation a meaning for us that our bosses and colleagues and employees might see very differently. Trust is difficult to sustain when we build a rich inner world of drama that we do not share with those around us. Put another way, trust is difficult to sustain when we are afraid to share our inner world; that's the only way to close the gap between what we're thinking and what others are thinking about what's real, not to mention what's smart, right, and fair.

The Power of One Word

Emotional threats send us into states of fear. In addition to picking up nonverbal threats, we can also be threatened by the power of one word. Words spoken by leaders in positions of authority carry greater weight in our minds than words spoken by those lower in the hierarchy. While neither Kathryn nor Margo could identify exactly when their relationship began to fall apart, it's likely that *a single conversation,* or even a single sentence, tipped them into distrust. Once we have a bad experience and begin to become distrustful of someone, that notion becomes embedded in our brain and can be difficult to dislodge. Unless we learn to hit those pause and rewind buttons to review exactly what happened, we can find ourselves in a situation similar to that of Kathryn and Margo.

The promising news is that if we learn to identify the signs of developing distrust before the amygdala is triggered, we can activate the higher-level brain functions in the executive brain, where empathy, judgment, and our more strategic social skills reside. When we learn to down-regulate, or reduce, the effects of fear, we can up-regulate, or increase, the impact of the executive brain. This helps us form social connections, strengthening our ability to bond with others instead of withdrawing from them. In fact, researchers have found that by learning to read the signals sent by the amygdala and head them off, we become far more effective at embracing trust—and we become more conversationally intelligent. We can learn to sideline signals from the amygdala by:

- Noticing how we react to threats—observing whether we go into "flight, fight, freeze, or appease."
- Labeling our reaction as normal.
- Noticing if we always choose the same reaction to threat (flight, fight, freeze, or appease) and noting how much the threat impacts us.
- Choosing an alternative way to react at the moment of contact (breathe in, breathe out; go into "discovery conversations"; share how you are feeling at the moment; stay calm and do nothing).
- Becoming more aware of our responses and realizing we can override our emotions and shift into other responses. We perceive what may happen before it happens and we interrupt that pattern.
- Transforming fear into trust, which is the heart of Conversational Intelligence.

Conversational Cocktails

Happily, strong bonds of trust serve up a cocktail of the brain's feel-good natural chemicals like oxytocin, dopamine, and serotonin. Put in practical terms, bonds of trust generate conversational cocktails that change neurochemistry and trigger the trust network in our brains. When we trust, we feel better and more positive. When we experience high levels of trust, we feel empowered to work out issues and challenges, open ourselves to new experiences, and link with others in a way that is sometimes called synchronicity.

At the Creating WE Institute, we have surveyed more than four thousand leaders across all industries and at all levels in their organizations. Through our research we have identified the two least-developed skills in the workplace: the *ability to have uncomfortable conversations* and the *ability to ask "what if" questions*. As you will see, both these skills are essential to building and sustaining trust, and to being candid and caring with one another. Many conversations are difficult. If we can't feel safe enough to have difficult conversations in an open and honest way, we will never get to a place where we can transform our culture.

Kathryn and Margo's story has a happy ending. I invited the two of them to meet me for coffee so I could share what I had learned, and I primed them for having the needed uncomfortable conversation. After we "deconstructed" the conversations they were having and they were able to see clearly that the root of their problem was the distrust triggered by their conversations, their communication breakdowns made sense to them and we began to make some progress in rebuilding trust.

Kathryn, for her part, shared that her best friends often call her out for her "incredulous" tone. In other words, her friends have found ways to let Kathryn know when she is sending nonverbal signals that turn people off. It may not be easy for her, but Kathryn is already learning to be more self-aware and to regulate her own behaviors. She also admitted to being under an unusual amount of stress, as senior management was pressing her for good results if she wanted to take the next step up the corporate ladder.

Margo, for her part, shared that she has always been "the sensitive one" in her family, and that it's not unlikely she might be reading too much into Kathryn's comments. She too is becoming more self-aware; in her case, she's noticing how often she chooses to negatively interpret events around her, to see them as threatening when they may not be. She is also learning to self-regulate her behavior, a vital step to managing fear and sustaining trust.

Resetting Relationships for Trust

I challenged Kathryn and Margo to hit the "reset" button on their relationship and return to the place where they trusted each other and could express their feelings without fear of recrimination or withdrawal. Kathryn pledged to create what I call "rules of engagement" within her organization (more on that in part 2 of this book), that allow employees like

Margo, regardless of their title, to not only be encouraged but rewarded for speaking up. Having seen things from Margo's point of view, Kathryn is working on being more attentive to the feelings of people who may be more sensitive than she. Margo is focusing on seeing the decent, stressed-out person behind Kathryn's spiky exterior, reminding herself that the woman she used to like so much is still there. The footnote to the story is that Margo not only kept her job, she eventually earned a promotion, thanks to the steps the two women took to rebuild the trust between them. And Kathryn was promoted too.

So what do great conversations look like? What would your organization look like if everyone knew and practiced the skills of Conversational Intelligence every day—and knew them so well that they could have a hand in building a great workplace and a high-performance organization? How do high levels of trust impact productivity and an organization's ability to achieve its goals and objectives? Even more importantly, how can trust change reality?

In the next chapter we'll focus on how to move from a devastating, unhealthy, difficult conversation to one that rebuilds trust and openness. This skill is vital in maintaining the relationships that are so important to us both at work and in our personal lives.

3

Moving from Distrust to Trust

Knowing others is intelligence; knowing yourself is true wisdom. Mastering others is strength; mastering yourself is true power.

—LAOZI

Life would be so simple if we had total control of what happens moment by moment in our lives. But the reality is, life is full of unexpected events, and many trigger us at a deep and visceral level. Let's look at one such stressful event and its ramifications, as well as some better ways of handling pressure-filled conversations.

You're sitting in a meeting with your team, brainstorming about a current financial crisis and what to do about it. Business is awful. People have stopped buying your products. Market share has plummeted overnight. You are scared. Others are scared. Everyone is throwing out ideas haphazardly. It's getting emotional. Some people are getting angry at one another. Others are closing down.

How often have you found yourself in situations like this? You want to support your team. You want to save the business. You are trying to navigate through the conversation and be helpful. It's confusing to keep track of what's going on. When you hear an idea you like or you see a possible opening to something new, you jump in and share it in the moment as it occurs to you. Then someone closes that door and says, "That's a stupid idea—we've tried that before and it failed."

As soon as you hear the word "stupid" and "failed" (even if it's implied rather than stated), you have an emotional reaction to the situation and the person. Instantaneously, the person you thought was on your side has become your archenemy. You got triggered. The colleague you thought was going to back you did not. He challenged you in front of others, and at a moment when you were vulnerable.

Something strange occurred, and a switch turned on in your brain. *You felt betrayed.* You looked your colleague in the eyes, as if to say, "Why now? Did you really mean what you said?" But you became silent as you pondered the thought: "Betrayed by a friend." You tune out of the meeting and ruminate. The team thinks you are still there. Your body is present, and your face may be making signs of listening, yet a big part of you has left the meeting.

Your body freezes up. You can't find words to respond. Your attention is now turned inside to your own silent conversation with yourself about being stupid and failing. You can't believe he said that to you. You were so sure of your opinion; it represented your "truth" and, up until this time, you trusted your gut. Yet in one moment you shifted your whole mind-set from *trust* to *distrust.*

Now, this story may seem exaggerated, but it's in fact a synthesis of hundreds of true stories that come from my coaching practice, and even from talking with strangers on trains and planes. The common theme that runs through all the stories is people believing they were in good stead with a colleague, only to find that when threatening dynamics were at play, the friend appeared to turn into a foe overnight.

Trust, as we have shown, has deep psychological and neurochemical roots. Trust and distrust happen as our inner and outer realities collide:

my own inner and outer reality and my reality with yours. We are more complex than we give ourselves credit for. Understanding our own complexity and drama is part of and vital to the story of trust and the power of Conversational Intelligence.

The Neuroscience of WE Triggers Empathy and Trust

When we are in a fear state, our conversations are shaped by the neurochemistry of fear. We can only think about protecting ourselves. The best antidotes to the brain's fear state are trust, empathy, and support. When someone shows concern for us, our brain chemistry makes a shift. We become calmer, we regain our composure, and we can begin once again to think in a constructive way. Because conversations depend on how we think, how we listen, and how we speak, it's vital that we learn to bring ourselves into a state of trust in order to ensure conversational success.

The Conversational Dashboard

The Conversational Dashboard™ is a visual representation of what happens in the brain during conversations. On the left are "Protect" behaviors and on the right are "Partner" behaviors. The left represents the primitive brain, where extreme fear and distrust reside, and the right represents the prefrontal cortex—or the executive brain—where our more advanced human capacities, such as trust, integrity, strategic thinking, and regulating emotions, reside. When we are confronted with a threatening situation—called an "amygdala hijack"—our brain floods with cortisol, a neurotransmitter that tells the brain to close down the executive functions, making them inaccessible even if the intention is there.

CONVERSATIONAL DASHBOARD™

FIGURE 3–1: Conversational Dashboard

Resistors and Experimentors

If you are a careful reader you might look at the Conversational Dashboard and think that I've misspelled Resistor and Experimentor. These are intentional spellings for my use of the terms. "Resistor" is the spelling used for an electrical component designed to introduce a known value of resistance into a circuit; "Experimentor" is "mentor of the experiment." These definitions represent how the Conversational Dashboard works. Conversations create electrical currents. Those that cause us to move into protective behavior are strong negative currents that trigger our primitive brain and cause a "flight, fright, freeze, or appease" response. By learning to mentor experimenting in our organizations, we activate a positive power that quells the brain's anxiety and fear and activates our executive brain's energy and capacity for co-creation.

Conversational Intelligence facilitates connectivity with others and enables us to activate our higher executive and human functions. When we use our Conversational Intelligence skills, the hormone oxytocin is released, among other neurotransmitters. Oxytocin is associated with bonding behaviors, and new research in neuroscience suggests that oxytocin may play a dominant role in the brain and the heart as a regulator of our need for social contact. Some scientists call oxytocin the "cuddle hormone," because it can create feelings of well-being as comforting as a mother's hug. This hormone's power may explain why loners die young, and why emotional rejection can be more painful than physical trauma.

So how can we activate oxytocin and trust even in the face of betrayal and distrust? How can we move from distrust to trust and change our conversational landscape?

Moving from Distrust to Trust

When my client Brenda began working for a global cosmetics company, she was taking a giant leap forward in her career. Not only was the new job a big promotion, she was also taking on responsibilities that cut across three functional areas. Her job was to bring together innovation, product development, and marketing, something that had never been done before at her new company. In many ways, she was brought in to lead a living supply chain experiment. The company gave her the opportunity to run a big department because she was so smart and had come with a strong background and broad experience. They also really liked her energy and leadership skills.

Brenda said yes to the opportunity because the job represented a new level of challenge as a leader and she had an appetite for growth. She had long been a high-potential leader, always moving up and getting results. This was the next step in her career, and she was eager to see what she could do.

We all join companies with the aspiration to do well, to make a contribution, and to bring value. We all want to be successful, respected, and admired by our colleagues and bosses. When we fail to perform, we get embarrassed or are fearful of looking bad, so we often resort to our primitive behaviors—hide, flee, fight, defend, or make others look bad to deflect the attention from ourselves. In other words, we start to live out of our hijacked amygdala.

It soon became apparent to Brenda that her new job was harder than she had imagined it would be. The company was forming matrix teams and cross-functional projects—and at the same time it was raising the bar on performance goals and the level of collaboration required. The environment became tense.

Brenda's previous job had been at a very large global company, where she was rewarded for her good judgment and decision making in the face of challenges. So, in her new position, she did what she had always done. She started to call the shots as she saw them. Giving instructions to people about how to do things came naturally to her. She had done some of these tasks before in her other company and so she applied her experience to this situation. What could have been easier? Then the walls came tumbling down—and they fell on Brenda, her direct reports, and her peers.

Our Brains Were Designed to Make Movies

When we join new companies, we bring not only our aspirations and our experience with us, we bring our old "movies" too. We store these movies and "how-tos" to help us in the future. Every time we have success with something we catalogue it and store it in our vault of memories (our limbic brain) along with how-tos we've learned along the way (stored in the neocortex). When the time comes, we pull out our "directory of insights and lessons learned" and put them into play in new situations. This is how the brain works.

How simple life would be if we could just do things the way we did them in the past. We can trust ourselves because we've seen it work. But often the techniques that were successful in the past don't apply to what appears to be a similar situation in the present.

Why? Because imposing our old solutions leaves out the differences between the old and the new situation: it leaves out the human factor, it leaves out others' experiences, and it leaves out the learning process in which others can get involved. People learn best by doing, not by being told what to do. The "my way or the highway" model of leadership fails to engage people in learning, and in many ways negates their experiences. When we rely on our previous knowledge and experiences to help us work out issues in the present, we often fall into the trap of doing more of the same thing, but getting worse results.

What Happens When the Leader Loses Power?

Brenda didn't see the problems coming, but within three months her employees started to distrust her leadership and question her good intentions. People felt she had her own agenda; she didn't listen and she made them feel stupid. Soon, Brenda's team turned against her. Trust between Brenda and her team was eroding day by day, and it took these forms:

- Fear of Brenda and fear of failure
- Higher levels of distrust in the team, brought on by Brenda's "power-over others" behaviors; her team believed she had an agenda, though in fact her intentions were principled
- Inability on the part of Brenda's staff to see how they could bring their insights and wisdom to the table; uncertainty and lack of quick answers to complex problems raised anxiety levels; the team wanted to conform to Brenda's leadership but when they tried they failed
- A feeling, by both Brenda and her team, that she thought she was right and they were wrong
- Prevalence of Groupthink—and the group thought that Brenda was wrong and the team was right; Brenda was now an outsider, and her team was coalescing against her

When Trust Is Gone, We Become Someone Else

The phrases "I've never acted that way before" and "This is not like me" describe Brenda's thoughts when she felt betrayed. She didn't feel like herself. She sometimes didn't like the way she talked to people, but she was chemically in a state of distrust and betrayal and didn't know what to do.

When our chemistry shifts from trust to distrust, and when we move further down the road to feeling betrayed, we can often show up at work as *someone else*. When fear masters us, we *are* someone else. Fear and conflict not only change our neural chemistry, they also change our persona and how others perceive us. In one nanosecond, we can move from being a trusted friend and advisor to someone others loathe and distrust.

Distrust	Trust
Distrust: When we are picking up any of the signals of distrust, our neurochemistry shifts. More likely than not, distrust produces:	**Trust:** When we are picking up any of the signals of trust our neurochemistry shifts. More likely than not, trust produces:
<ul><li>Higher levels of cortisol and the presence of catecholamine, which closes down our prefrontal cortex, where new ideas, creative thinking, empathy, and good judgment reside</li><li>Changes in the dACC (dorsal anterior cingulate cortex), a part of the brain that is sensitive to conflict; this center responds by sending signals to the amygdala to take over and protect</li><li>Higher levels of testosterone, which makes us more aggressive and induces us to fight to protect our territory</li><li>Higher levels of norepinephrine, which cause us to want to think more negative thoughts and want to fight</li></ul>	<ul><li>Higher levels of dopamine—happy hormone—which gives us a positive outlook (cup half full) and assigns good feelings to our interactions; we have more positive memories to look back on and more positive views of the future</li><li>Higher levels of oxytocin—a bonding hormone—which makes us feel closer to others and want to be with them and be open with them</li><li>Higher levels of endorphins, which makes us feel good, and feel more excited</li><li>Higher levels of serotonin, which also makes us feel good</li></ul>

Trust Attempts Backfiring

Brenda was unable to talk with her team directly and the team wasn't able to talk with her about all the issues that were emerging, so the company created an "Onboarding Intervention" to allow people to share what was on their minds. The goal was to open a dialogue and get the issues on the table, yet there was no priming, no preparation, and no framing that would permit trust to emerge (more on this subject in chapter 9, "A Toolkit for Level III Conversations"). As the session evolved, it became clear that team members had made up their minds about Brenda—they had gone up what I call the Ladder of Conclusions™.

LADDER OF CONCLUSIONS™

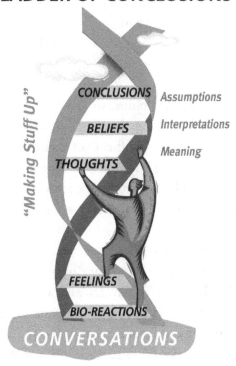

FIGURE 3–2: Ladder of Conclusions

We read the ladder from the bottom up, starting with "Conversations." From the moment of contact, bio-reactions occur at the chemical level; our reactions proceed to the cognitive level, where we are entrenched in our point of view and "attached to being right."

1. **Bio-reactions:** Conversations take place at the chemical level first and fastest—judgments are made within .07 seconds. Cortisol or oxytocin may go up; our hearts may beat faster. The reaction at the moment of contact activates a network, either the "protect/fear network" or the "trust network."

2. **Feelings:** We label our interaction either "feel good" or "feel bad." This translates into a judgment about whether the person we're speaking with is a friend or a foe, with the corresponding judgment: I can trust you or I can't.

3. **Thoughts:** As we move up the ladder to the thought level we put words to our feelings—we make meaning (often, we are making stuff up).

4. **Beliefs:** Once we make up our story, or create meaning, we pull in other beliefs we have about this situation or person; we draw from our past experience and we affirm our thoughts.

5. **Conclusions:** When we have reached "Conclusions," we block out a lot of other people's opinions. We stop seeing or hearing other points of view. We may even move into a state of denial.[1]

Once we make up our minds about someone we set out to *prove we are right.* When we are addicted to being right, we are mastered by our amygdala—specifically the "fight" behaviors, and we see the world through an I-centric point of view. This was the case with Brenda. Her team didn't trust her, and she didn't trust them.

The Onboarding Intervention turned into a venting and dumping session, with the whole room taking sides, and most labeling her as a non-collaborative, dictatorial leader. As you'll learn in the next section, Brenda was stuck in extreme Level II: positional interaction dynamics. She was fighting for her position and the team members were fighting for theirs. Rather than using the session to seek better ways of working together, to build trust and understanding, and to transform their perspectives, they used it to reinforce their preconceived notions.

The meeting failed to bring harmony and understanding. But the problems went deeper than that. Brenda felt betrayed by her team. None of them had talked with her directly about her leadership style. No one had given her feedback that she was pushing too hard or being too direct for her new company's culture. Had she gotten that feedback she might have put her energy into better fitting into the culture. But everyone went radio silent until the big intervention, and then, in front of all her direct reports, she felt like she was being publicly assassinated. Brenda had no one to confide in and no one to hold up a mirror so she could see the truth reflected back. She was thrown off her game and started to make movies in her head about who might have caused these problems for her.

She identified two people—one on her team and one peer—who might have been the origins of her now deep and painful wounds. Brenda was a tough executive, so she kept moving forward and doing her job, yet she could feel the groundswell around her.

Her relationships with the two people she'd identified as the troublemakers became even more strained, as she was unable to find words to talk with these people directly. She couldn't put her arms around the "truth" any more. She just knew her team and her peers had betrayed her, and she tried her best to act natural and to grin and bear it.

Within eight months, everyone's frustration had bubbled to the top; complaints made their way to HR, and I was bought in as Brenda's executive coach.

Re-stor(y)ing Trust

By the time I began as Brenda's executive coach, she'd been with the company for a year and a half. That's a long time for problems to fester. She didn't want or expect the feedback she got from her team, and their comments profoundly affected her spirits and perspective. In the eight months after the Onboarding Intervention, Brenda retreated mentally and emotionally, trying to work with her "enemies" and find a way to rebuild trust. Our coaching was designed to help her start over, to deconstruct the conversations, uncover where they went wrong, and come up with ways to regain trust with her team and peers. As we worked on building trust, we would also look to shape effective leadership strategies for the future.

Over the course of the next six months we worked on self-awareness, leadership assessments, and gaining new insights into the past, present, and future. Through my 360-interview process and Conversational Intelligence framework we learned more about "her story" and "their story," and started to examine the dynamics and decide what to do about them.

When we feel we *can't trust* someone who is key to our success and the company's success we can easily retreat into a world of interpretation to give us a sense that "I'm okay." To feel whole again, we make up stories—our own stories. In this state of defensiveness, my story and yours will almost never agree. In my story, you are to blame; in your story, I am to blame.

As a key part of our coaching process, I worked with Brenda to help her move out of her head, where she was hijacked by her *fear networks*—her stories and the drama that drove her to distrust her team—and guided her back into reality, where her *trust networks* would flourish and she could learn to have open and trusting conversations with each person.

At each session, Brenda and I focused on trust and betrayal issues one step at a time, and after each session she was to do exercises to practice her newfound trust skills. It was more than skill building that made a difference for Brenda and her team. She was able to use the TRUST Model to build a new movie and a new reality with her team.

Applying the TRUST Model to Everyday Life

I introduced the TRUST Model to Brenda and we used it as a "road map" that would help her move forward one step at a time. Here is the plan of action Brenda followed.

The TRUST Model is made up of five steps a leader can take to restore trust. These are some of the most powerful skills a leader can learn—they can transform an executive's trajectory, as they did for Brenda. Each step provides a way to signal our brains to move into higher levels of trust.

Step into Trust with:	Refocus on Actions That Build and Sustain Trust
Step 1 *Transparency* *Through Quelling Fear*	***Take the lead.*** Quell the amygdala by talking about the threats and fears that are standing in the way of building trust. Be open and communicate with others to share and quell threats. This sends messages of trust that the amygdala understands: "I trust you will not harm me." ***Refocus*** on quelling the reptilian brain (amygdala) by shaping the conversations to talk openly about the threats and fears that are standing in the way of building trust. Open, candid, and caring conversations send messages of trust.
Step 2 *Relationship* *Through heart coherence*	***Take the lead.*** Extend the olive branch, even with people you may see as foes. Connect and engage in building relationships. Extending trust sends messages of friendship that shift the energy toward appreciation. Heart appreciation shifts our attention and intention to seek connectivity, reduces the fear of power-over energy, and builds power-with connectivity.

Step into Trust with:	Refocus on Actions That Build and Sustain Trust
	Refocus on engaging the heart brain by shaping the conversation to extend trust and by sending messages of appreciation to others. When we refocus on heart appreciation we create higher levels of heart coherence, which enables us to activate the wisdom of the five brains.
Step 3 *Understanding* *Through sharing and understanding needs and emotions*	*Take the lead.* Be inclusive. Invite people into the inner circle. Talk openly about needs and aspirations. Reframe and relabel uncomfortable conversations as opportunities to get to know what's on each other's minds. Listening with this focus in mind and heart opens new channels of communication and quells doubts about "where I fit in." This moves us from states of distrust of others' intentions toward understanding and trusting each other. *Refocus* on engaging the limbic brain by inviting others to be included openly in conversation about their needs and emotions. Stepping into each other's shoes and seeing the world from another's eyes validates the other person's worldview.
Step 4 *Shared Success* *Through opening minds to others and creating strategies for mutual success*	*Take the lead.* Have conversations that focus on mutual success. Lower your attachment to being right and shift the conversation from entrenchment to discovery. Look at what success means from each other's point of view and build benchmarks for measuring success; focus on co-creating what success looks like with others. *Refocus* on engaging the neocortex by shaping conversations to enable you to put issues and conflicts on the table without fear of reappraisal and retribution. Weave deeper threads of trust into the relationship.

Step into Trust with:	Refocus on Actions That Build and Sustain Trust
Step 5 **Testing Assumptions & Telling the Truth** *Through truth, empathy, and judgment*	***Take the lead.*** Test perceptions and assumptions about reality. Focus on closing the gaps between what you expect and what you get with others. Step into each other's shoes, and see the world from the other person's perspectives—the highest level of trust that we humans are able to experience together. Then truth can be discovered together— and one view of the world emerges. ***Refocus*** on engaging the prefrontal cortex—the executive brain—by shaping conversations that let you step into each other's shoes and see the world from another's perspective.

Step 1: Transparency

Our first sessions were designed to make threats transparent and to minimize their impact. Being able to talk about our frustrations and worries openly, without fear of retribution, is the first step toward building and sustaining trust.

> *BrainTrust:* An assurance of Transparency quells the reptilian brain, or primitive brain, which reacts to fear, threat, and loss.

When we learn to create the conditions for quelling fear we encourage people to talk openly about the threats and fears that are standing in the way of building trust. In doing this, we begin the process of reconnecting with others, and trust emerges. *Transparency is also about sharing our intentions so people don't read into them.*

ACTIONS: Brenda chose a few people with whom she had a distrustful relationship and began the slow process of having intentional, open, candid, and caring conversations. She started with the easier relationships and practiced talking openly, giving healthy feedback, and showing respect and appreciation. Her direct reports, who had felt she didn't respect them, became open to rebuilding trust. As you are learning, distrust and fear originate in our reptilian brain, particularly the amygdala. Before moving on to the next level, Brenda had to let people feel safe with her—get them to realize she was not going to fire them—and let them know that she wanted to be on their side, helping them succeed.

Step 2: Relationships

Focusing on building relationships with her peers and direct reports was a big milestone for Brenda. In our next sessions we worked on strategies for rebuilding those relationships characterized by distrust.

> *BrainTrust:* Building relationships activates the heart brain, which reacts to signals of "friend or foe" from others. Can I trust this person to have my best interest at heart?

Brenda had a "driving personality." She set goals and pushed her people to meet them, and was less than supportive when they failed. "Task before relationship" was her mantra, but this philosophy didn't mesh well with her new company's relationship-driven culture.

ACTIONS: With each of her key direct reports, Brenda had what I call Partnering Conversations, which you will learn how to do later in the book. These conversations shift relationships from judgment to respect and create the conditions and agreements that allow people to work together productively. This tool provides a road map for difficult conversations and lays out how to rebuild or expand trust.

By doing an exercise that focused on "what works for you and what works for me" conversations, Brenda learned a lot about her people and their needs. The knowledge she gained showed her how to best lead her organization forward.

What a reversal. As Brenda became open to getting to know each of her direct reports and peers *personally*, something shifted. People stopped feeling she was a "power-over others" leader and learned to work with her as a "power-with others" leader. They felt appreciated, and Brenda began consciously sending messages of trust—messages that she was a friend, not a foe—which calms anxiety about being appreciated. This enabled her to connect with others, and to get to know them personally.

As you are learning, our heart energy contributes deeply to the story of trust, and Brenda was making heart connections that she had never made before. She felt an opening up of her heart and of her mind. She found her interest in others' well-being becoming stronger. What quells the brain's fear state is trust, empathy, and support, and Brenda was feeling those emotions in ways she hadn't felt before. When people are connecting, they are syncing at an energetic level. Mirror neurons, located right below the prefrontal cortex, are firing off, forming a bridge of empathy and insight with others. We activate our ability for higher levels of bonding, collaborating, and experiencing high-point moments with others, which means that the levels of oxytocin are increasing as we interact—this influx of neurochemicals reinforces trust.

Step 3: Understanding

The next sessions with Brenda centered on ensuring she learned more about what was really on people's minds—she needed to learn to see the world through their eyes, not only her own. Once we understand how to stand in another's shoes and understand his perspective, we are in a better position to honor each other. I believe understanding means we "stand under" the same view of the world. People trust us more when we have their best interest at heart. Understanding each other's "context" and "perspective" is invaluable for building trust. *Listening to how another person "holds his reality"—and doing it without judgment—is priceless.*

BrainTrust: Our limbic brain helps create Understanding by storing memories of all our interactions; we sort these memories along the lines of whether they "feel good" or "feel bad." Our limbic brain plays a big role in helping us know whom we can trust and whom we cannot by sending out the chemical messages that encourage us to open up to others or to close down. The limbic brain also functions as our memory vault. We store memories of all the people we have met and of all the social interactions we have. We learn to assess whether we fit in—whether we feel we belong—and that feeling of belonging is critical to mental health. Human beings are tribal. Being a part of the tribe is essential for mental health.

ACTIONS: Through her challenging onboarding process, Brenda realized she felt like an outcast. She realized that even leaders need to feel that they belong and that they *fit into the tribe.* On reflection, she saw that she *had* fit in at her previous company and she came to understand why she wasn't fitting in now. Through Step III of the TRUST process, Brenda gained insights that changed her state of mind and enabled her to connect with others. She realized that when she was uncertain about her role as a leader, she would turn to *power-over others* leadership behaviors, damaging her relationships even more. By claiming her throne, she put distance between herself and others. The TRUST process allowed her to see strategies for building "power-with others" relationships, an insight that changed her life forever.

Step 4: Shared Success

Brenda was making headway. In our next sessions we worked to ensure she was creating a shared vision of success with others. When we have a common view of success we start to intuitively trust that others will make decisions similar to ours, and we trust they will work out conflicts fairly.

BrainTrust: Our neocortex functions to help us build and shape strategies for success. When we are attached to being right and advocate our point of view over all others, we give the impression we "have an agenda." Entrenchment in our point of view leads to distrust, driving conversations that elicit protective behavior. *We can't persuade someone to want our success—that only creates resistance.*

ACTIONS: Brenda was learning that sharing a vision for success with others weaves deeper threads of trust in relationships. Once she had success with the easier relationships she was stronger and more prepared to have heart-to-heart conversations with those she felt had betrayed her and whom she now distrusted. It was as though Brenda was building her trust muscles for what would come next: face-to-face truth telling and building empathy and partnership in a sustained way.

Step 5: Testing Assumptions and Truth-Telling

Brenda was now experiencing feelings about her team she had never felt before, and she was having new insights about her betrayers that enabled her to see the possibility that she might be able to start over with a fresh slate.

BrainTrust: Researchers have discovered that once we have been betrayed we label the betrayer a foe. If we experience multiple instances of betrayal with the same person, we will mentally and even physically respond to that person as a foe. When this happens, our brains go into a different gear, and not only do we have pain from our encounters with the betrayer, we also seek retribution.

ACTIONS: Brenda's betrayal never went that far, fortunately. By working to rebuild trust, however, she did experience a positive shift she described thus: "It is like something switched in my brain. I am now able to see the bigger picture. I'm not attached to being right. I can see how this problem happened and it's not about finding fault." She was able to see everything in a totally new way.

She said it felt like her mind was opening up to new insights and levels of awareness she had never felt before. She was able to access the truth (truth-telling starts with being able to see the truth about our own behavior). Her mind's movies changed; how she thought about others changed. She began to test her assumptions about "friend or foe," and people who had been foes were now starting to show up as colleagues. She was able to let go of her old assumptions and build new contexts and frameworks that included people as part of her inner circle rather than left them outside as enemies. Our conversations are a reflection of our state of mind. Brenda was now able to connect with people differently—and her conversations reflected this new insight.

In our next sessions we talked more about differences of opinion and about working out conflicts with empathy and compassion. As Brenda learned the higher-level skills of truth telling, having empathy for others, and checking her assumptions at the door, she really got at the heart of trust and was able to engage more fully and more openly with others.

Is Our Heart a Brain?

As we discussed earlier, the part of the brain that helps to elevate us to higher levels of empathy and to have good judgment even in the face of conflict is the prefrontal cortex, working in concert with the rest of the brain, specifically the heart brain.

There is a lot of controversy about whether the heart is a "brain." In my work, I include the heart as an actual brain. It works in concert with the other brains, and its impact on our ability to connect, engage, and access the prefrontal cortex has been demonstrated. What we are learning is that the heart's electrical patterns send messages to the brain, signaling the brain to either open up or close down. Research by the Institute of HeartMath has shown that when our heart beats in a coherent pattern we feel safe, and

THE HEART BRAIN

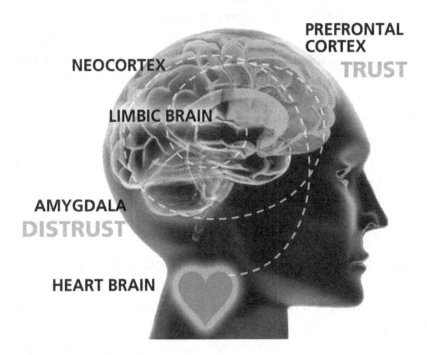

FIGURE 3–3: The Heart Brain

the message to the brain is to open up. When the heart pattern is incoherent and erratic, we feel unsafe, and the prefrontal cortex closes down.

Understanding these two patterns—heart coherence or lack of coherence—is vital to understanding how to get to Level III and how to get unstuck from Levels I and II. The heart brain is pivotal to understanding the Wisdom of the Five Brain Model, which we'll talk about more in chapter 5.

When leaders learn to use the TRUST Model effectively, they strengthen their "BrainTrust" and:

- Create **Transparency,** which signals "safety" to the reptilian brain (amygdala)

- Focus on **Relationships** first to connect with others, which signals "friend" not "foe." This signals the heart brain that it's okay to connect, and people get into sync or become open to building rapport.
- Focus on building **Understanding** and seeing the world from another's eyes. This calms the limbic brain, enhancing bonding and creating the feeling that "we're all in this together."
- Focus on creating **Shared success** for the future—a shared view of mutual success. Our neocortex is able to put words and pictures to what success looks like, signaling the prefrontal cortex that it's safe to open up.
- Focus on **Truth telling and testing assumptions** (candor and caring), which builds and expands trust.

These five steps trigger the trust networks located in the prefrontal cortex and help us access Conversational Intelligence. By taking these steps, we activate and co-create brain connections in the trust network. By learning to see the world from another's perspective, we can attain the highest level of trust. But Brenda was not finished yet. She moved forward into trust and met with her two toughest critics.

What Was Missing

Confronting others openly, honestly, and directly when we feel betrayed seems like an almost impossible task. When trust is lost, we don't recover quickly. We ruminate and we gossip with others to try to make sense of who is to blame. In the worst-case scenarios, we feel a desire for retribution and actually look for chances to get even with the person who betrayed us.

Brenda felt the groupthink emerge around her at the Onboarding Intervention. She felt alone and unprepared to defend herself. It's easy to open up when others in the room are on your side. When groupthink and "us–them" relationships emerge, we stand alone and afraid. Brenda saw she was alone. Everyone involved in the onboarding process—all the other executives—had concluded she was the problem. Confronting others individually or in a group requires that we focus on making it safe to be transparent. When we share in building the relationship, with both parties feeling the power of the exchange, a power-with relationship evolves. When we feel others want to own us or own our power—which is a power-over relationship—we fear harm and cannot open up with honesty. If we think of our conversations as a power-over experience, it's impossible to be comfortable confronting others honestly.

Additionally, confronting another person with difficult conversations brings up potentially volatile emotions, so we move with caution and keep our real feelings close to our chest. In the most extreme cases, when we are faced with situations that stir up highly charged emotional content, most of the tension and drama is actually taking place in our own minds. This is our "story;" it is how we create meaning and explain the drama of our experience and our emotions. Emotions are one way the brain processes without language. Much of our frustration comes from trying to find the right words to explain something we are feeling when what we have to say is complex. Shifting from feelings to words is often a big leap... and one that takes Conversational Intelligence to execute. Yet behind the scenes is the reality of the challenge: even though it's not easy, how do we communicate with each other and have healthy conversations when we feel we are pushed to the edge? How do we deal with others in a way that builds relationships rather than erodes them? How do we masterfully keep ourselves in a state of openness, with our assumptions and inferences in check?

Candor, collaboration, and cooperation are almost impossible to establish in environments where turf wars and one-upsmanship exist. No one wants to lose. Competition is ingrained in our corporate culture. Trust does not come easily when we feel someone—maybe even a friend—might be out for our job.

When we are conscious of the meta-messages, we can create a safe environment for open, candid, caring conversations that allow both parties to open up, to share, and to interact at the highest trust levels possible. When we begin to confront *threatening* topics openly in our conversations and test our assumptions so we don't draw conclusions, everything changes.

Sharing our deepest perspectives, feelings, and aspirations is a human need. It is how we learn and grow, and it's how we connect with and validate each other. In doing these things, we evolve our insights and wisdom to a higher level.

Shifting from I to WE

As Brenda learned, trust is something that happens between people and inside of us. We need to bridge our outer spaces and our inner spaces to ensure trust is alive for both parties. Here is a list that summarizes the "I to WE" shift.

- **T—Transparency (Language of the reptilian brain)**
  - *I-centric:* Secrecy; closed doors; threats; lack of clarity; lack of alignment
  - *WE-centric:* Openness; sharing of threats, intentions, aspirations, and objectives; movement toward establishing common, aligned objectives

- **R—Relationships (Language of the heart brain)**
  - *I-centric:* Rejection; resistance; retribution; adversarial relationships; suspicion
  - *WE-centric:* Respect; rapport; caring; candor; nonjudgmental listening to deeply connect and build partnership

- **U—Understanding (Language of the limbic brain)**
  - *I-centric:* Uncertainty; focus on tasks; unrealistic expectations; disappointment; judgment

- *WE-centric:* Understanding; ability to stand in each other's shoes; empathy for others' "context"; seeing and understanding (or standing under) another perspective of reality; partnership; support

- S—Shared Success (Language of the neocortex)
  - *I-centric:* Promotion of self-interest; focus on "I" and "me"; seeking of personal recognition and reward
  - *WE-centric:* Bonding with others to create a vision of shared success; building of a shared vision that holds the space for a bigger framework for mutual success; pursuit of shared interests and celebration of shared successes

- T—Testing Assumptions and Truth-Telling (Language of the prefrontal cortex)
  - *I-centric:* Reactions of anger, anxiety, withdrawal, resignation
  - *WE-centric:* Regular, open, and nonjudgmental discussion of assumptions and disappointments as part of collaborative problem solving; identification and discussion of "reality gaps" and effort to close the gaps for mutual success; willingness to start over again if distrust emerges

In the next chapter, we'll talk about conversational rituals and blind spots. Chapter 4 will help you build your Third Eye, a hyperawareness of the link between your intentions and their impact during conversations. You'll learn how to elevate your awareness to see more and strategically focus your attention on navigating with others even in the most difficult conversations.

PART II

Raising Your Conversational Intelligence

4

Challenges of Navigating
the Conversational Highway

*To get to the next level of greatness depends on the quality of the culture,
which depends on the quality of the relationships, which depends on the
quality of the conversations. Everything happens through conversations!*

—JUDITH E. GLASER

I've come to treasure the insight that conversations are "rituals" we embed into our culture and our relationships, and which give us a way to successfully structure our engagements with others. In this part of the book, we'll focus on what you can do to shape conversations for success.

As an organizational anthropologist, I have been a student of conversational rituals my whole life. Whether it is bowing slightly to someone when greeting her or passing the peace pipe at a campfire or taking the time to introduce people in a room before the conversation begins, each ritual has a place and each enhances or impedes communication and engagement. Rituals, however, are more than what we do to start a conversation. They are the very architecture of conversations. Conversational rituals are what we do when we talk.

This part of the book will help you identify the rituals and practices you need to architect conversations for mutual success by bringing out the best each person has to offer. These practices work in one-to-one relationships, they work in teams, and they work in larger organizational transformations. They work because they influence our behavior at the neurochemical level. They work because this is where all human beings are alike—it's how we are hardwired and it's what makes us human.

Conversational rituals differentiate humans from other species and enable us to develop and handle complexity, ambiguity, and change. They allow us to evolve and grow—they are the tools we use to teach ourselves and one another what we know and to raise us up to learn what we don't know. Conversational rituals allow us to build common languages, definitions, and meanings that in turn create community. We have evolved conversational rituals to strengthen our world, so whatever part of the world you live in, these practices will work.

My Mind-Opening Experiment

Three decades ago I started one of my first experiments in Conversational Intelligence. I was solving a problem for a client, and from this simple yet elegant experiment I gained profound insights that would become vital to the work I do today.

My "subjects" were seventeen high-powered sales executives from Union Carbide who feared they would lose a bid for a key contract. They brought me in to figure out how they could raise their game and beat out the other seven competitors.

I charted their interactions for more than two weeks. As they did what I called "real-plays"—that is, re-created their conversations with customers—their patterns of interaction became clear. Over the course of my observations, I saw that 85 percent of the time these executives were using statements and 15 percent of the time they were asking questions. Almost all of those questions were statements in disguise. What I realized was that the sales executives had become bound by conversational rituals that were not serving them very well—and they were not alone.

Many people fall into this conversational pattern when they are trying to convince someone of their point of view. Untrained and unaware salespeople do it a lot. They talk and then talk more to ensure that the other person gets the point. Their focus is almost exclusively on telling others what's on their minds or trying to persuade others that their views are right, thinking this is a good conversation.

By learning how to change their conversational rituals—their interaction dynamics—the Union Carbide team improved their presentation and won the contract, creating a long-term customer in the process!

Almost three decades later, and after thousands of hours observing executives interacting in situations such as prospecting, developing businesses, reviewing their employees, leading teams, launching new initiatives, and encouraging innovation, I still see similar results. When we create conversational rituals that enable us to honor and respect others' views of the world—especially when these views are very different from our own—*we create a space* for better conversations and for new ideas to emerge. Today I call this most evolved form of Conversational Intelligence Level III interaction dynamics, or transformational conversations. These are Co-creating Conversations in which both people are transforming each other's thoughts, ideas, and belief systems. In many cases, the transformational process enables both people to better match and align a shared picture of "reality" using Conversational Intelligence practices to get there.

Blind Spots That Limit Our Sight

Conversational rituals can be I-centric, like persuading someone until she gives in or intimidating someone before a negotiation so he gives up more than he'd planned. Conversational rituals can also be

WE-centric—like shaking hands to greet someone before a difficult conversation or making up after an argument. All of these conversational rituals define how we engage with others, and they make up our culture, "how we do things around here."

What I also learned, and what I can now demonstrate with the help of neuroscience, is that while conversational rituals are designed to help us connect more fully with others, human beings have conversational blind spots. These are beliefs that get in the way of us connecting mind to mind with others, and where we have blind spots, we also have conflicts and breakdowns.

Breakdowns happen when you and I think we are talking to each other but we are really talking past each other. We are so engrossed in what we have to say that we don't realize we are carrying on our own monologues, not dialogues. When we are conversationally blind, our conversations often go off track because we see the world from our own perspective and not from the other person's.

Five Conversational Blind Spots

How do we become more conversationally intelligent? One way to improve is by recognizing and overcoming the five most common conversational blind spots.

Blind Spot #1

The first blind spot involves an assumption that others see what we see, feel what we feel, and think what we think. Backstory: When we are engrossed and attached to our point of view, we are unable to connect with others' perspectives. If we did, we would realize how differently they see the world. Yet our bodies pick up the lack of connectivity and switch on a stronger need to persuade others we are right. Human beings actually have a high addiction to being right.

When we persuade others we are right, our dopamine level goes up. It's like a natural high—dopamine is part of the brain's reward center. *Winning a point makes us feel good—it makes others feel bad, but we often don't realize that.*

Blind Spot #2

Blind Spot #2 is the failure to realize that fear, trust, and distrust changes how we see and interpret reality, and therefore how we talk about it. Backstory: When in a state of fear, we release cortisol and catecholamines, which closes down the prefrontal cortex. We feel threatened, move into protective behaviors, and often don't even realize we are doing it.

Blind Spot #3

An inability to stand in each other's shoes when we are fearful or upset characterizes Blind Spot #3. Backstory: Researchers in Parva, Italy, led by Giacomo Rizzolatti discovered, through their 1999 research on monkeys (and later humans), that our brain has unique neurons called mirror neurons. These neurons give us a view into what others feel, think, and intend. When we listen deeply, turn off our judgment mechanisms, and allow ourselves to connect with others, we are activating the mirror neuron system, now thought of as "having empathy for others." Yet when we are fearful, that power to connect becomes disconnected, and our sensitivity to others' perspectives recedes.

Blind Spot #4

Blind Spot #4 is the assumption that we remember what others say, when we actually remember what we think about what others say. Backstory: Researchers have concluded two things. One is that we drop out of conversations every twelve to eighteen seconds to process what people are saying; two, we often remember what we think about what another person is saying because that is a stronger internal process and chemical signal. In other words, *our internal listening and dialogue trumps the other person's speech.*

Blind Spot #5

The assumption that *meaning* resides in the speaker, when in fact it resides in the listener, characterizes Blind Spot #5. Backstory: For me to make meaning I need to draw out what I think you are saying from my vault of experiences, specifically from the hippocampus, where memory is stored in the limbic system, or emotional brain; or I may draw from the neocortex, where I store memories of what to do and how to do it. My brain will pull the meaning from my experiences and I then *bring them into the conversation* to make sense of what I hear. That's why "in my mind's eye" I can see a totally different picture of what you are saying than what your mind sees. Meaning resides in the listener until the speaker takes the time to validate and link back to make sure both have the same picture and shared meaning.

Bridging Our Reality Gaps

Our blind spots spring from reality gaps. Your reality and mine are not the same. You and I have different experiences, we know different people, we came from different parts of the world, and we use different language to label our world. Even those of us who are in the same room at the same time will take away different impressions of our time together. That is why culture is so important. It creates the conversational rituals and practices that harmonize our experiences, create a shared language, and help us bridge and connect with others more fully—it creates a shared reality.[1]

Too often we fail to recognize or acknowledge that our reality is not the same as the reality of the person we are speaking with. Through coaching, the Union Carbide sales team learned to use the term "reality gaps," and learned to make their invisible blind spots visible. They began to notice when they were making assumptions, interpreting incorrectly, and jumping to conclusions.

The team learned to ask discovery questions—questions *for which you have no answers.* When they began to ask the right questions, they were able to learn about and map their customer's mind-set, which enabled them to gain new insights about their customer's needs, needs they'd previously been blind to.

Open-Ended Questions

What I discovered as I watched the Union Carbide executives, as well as thousands of others from every company I visit, is that people start by asking questions that have a yes or no answer. For example, an executive might ask, "You should do 'x,' don't you think?" This is a Level I question. The question is not provocative, which is a quality of Level II questions, or catalytic, which is characteristic of Level III questions. It's really a statement in disguise.

My goal with all my clients is to help them ask the highest form of questions, which I call discovery questions. These questions open our minds to explore new avenues of thought with each other. They help us enter each other's worlds, navigate each other's thoughts and feelings, and open and harvest new insights and wisdom not yet explored by either person.

Following are examples of Level I, Level II, and Level III questions that show how the same issue is handled in different ways via different levels of questions. Note that all of these are questions for which there are no expected answers.

Level I:
- Are you okay with taking the second writing sample to add to our marketing materials?

Level II:
- I'm fascinated by the second sample. It's got all the qualities of great writing. How are you thinking about it? Can you join me

in this decision? Is anything stopping you from getting on board with this?

Level III:
- Which of the writing samples will achieve the best outcomes for our sales promotion and marketing?
- What assumptions do you hold about the project's success that we should consider as we have the conversation?
- How would you describe success in this situation?
- Are there any *feared implications* that we should consider and talk more about before we decide?

Once team members had become sensitized to the different types of questions and understood that they could relate to their customers' mind-sets through Level III questions, the Union Carbide team began to engage with their customers through empathy. They were able to step into their customers' shoes and experience their challenges and frustrations from a totally different point of view, a customer-centric point of view. At that point, the customers began to feel that the salespeople were no longer simply trying to sell them; customers felt that the Union Carbide team understood their challenges and were willing to work as a partner in solving them. By changing their interaction dynamics from Level I (tell/ask) through Level II (advocate/inquire) to Level III (share/discover), Union Carbide was able to win the contract and create a long-term customer.

Gauging Results with a Conversational Dashboard

We know now that conversational blind spots can emerge without us even realizing it, so how do we know we are having the best possible conversations? How do we know whether our conversations are leading to transformational results?

CONVERSATIONAL DASHBOARD™

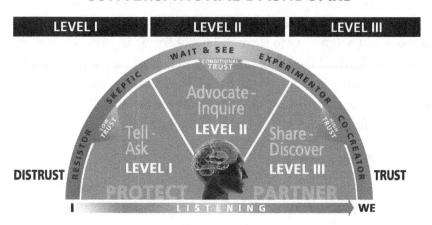

FIGURE 4–1: Conversational Dashboard

Following is a great conversational tool I call the Conversational Dashboard. It enables you to recognize the quality of your interaction dynamics, the level of trust you and others are operating with, and the outcomes produced by each level of conversation. As you learn to use the Conversational Dashboard, you can begin to eliminate Conversational Intelligence blind spots and engage in healthy conversations at Levels I, II, and III.

Level I: Transactional

Conversations often can be categorized as "Tell and Ask" interaction dynamics. People are exchanging information, updates, and facts that help us align our realities or confirm we are on the same page. There is not a lot of trust, and people are focusing more on what they need to get from each other to validate and confirm their view of reality.

Level II: Positional

These conversations are characterized by "Advocate and Inquire" inter-action dynamics. In a Level II conversation, I am advocating for what I want (not just telling you) and I am inquiring about your beliefs so I can influence you to my point of view. Trust is conditional. If I feel you have my back and will not try to steamroll me or win at all costs, I will move into higher levels of trust. However, if I feel that you are not going to be fair or are lobbying at my expense, I will retreat into protective behaviors. Conditional trust raises the levels of uncertainty, which can also trigger the fear networks (Can I open up or not? Can I trust or not?).

Level III: Transformational

Transformational conversations are marked by "Share and Discover" interaction dynamics. When I share first, my brain receives a cue that I will be vulnerable with you and that I will open up my inner thoughts, ideas, and feelings. Others in the conversation receive the signal that you are willing to be influenced, that you care about them, and that they can trust you to experiment and innovate with them. As we share and discover, we become "mentors of the experiment," and we will be able to co-create with one another to achieve greater shared success—far beyond what we ever imagined.

Conversational Intelligence™ Matrix

What Do We Exchange?	LEVEL I TRANSACTIONAL "Exchange Information" TELL ASK	LEVEL II POSITIONAL "Exchange Power" ADVOCATE INQUIRE	LEVEL III TRANSFORMATIONAL "Exchange Energy" SHARE DISCOVER
Interaction Dynamics	Ask-Tell	Advocate-Inquire	Share-Discover
Space	Closes Spaces	Limits Space	Creates Space
Focus	Giving and taking information	Exploring others' positions seeking a win-win solution	Exploring others' perspectives; joining and transforming reality; innovating
Blindspots & Overuse	"Tell-Sell-Yell Syndrome" Tendency toward telling more than asking	"Addicted to Being Right" Tendency to ask questions for which you have all the answers	"All Talk No Action" Tendency for too much talk and no action
INTENTION	**INFORM**	**PERSUADE**	**CO-CREATE**
Listen	To protect	To accept or reject	To connect
I-WE	I-centric	I & We-centric	WE-centric
Success	My success	Win at all cost	Mutual success
Trust	Low trust	Conditional trust	High trust
Influence	Not open to influence	Desire to influence	Open to influence
Skills to Develop	Ability to ask open ended questions and foster 'give and take'	Ability to share the conversational space with others; expand power	Ability to ask questions for which you have no answers; co-creating

CONVERSATIONAL INTELLIGENCE™

Closing the Reality Gap

To raise your Conversational Intelligence (C-IQ) you need to become master and creator—or better yet, co-creator—of conversational rituals that enable the greatest expression of ideas, feelings, hunches, thoughts, and aspirations possible. Once you learn these skills and tools, you can masterfully shape the conversational space and begin to experience the power of Conversational Intelligence.

Next, we'll dive deeper into the neuroscience behind Level I, II, and III interaction dynamics and see how they work to open up or close down our brains during conversations.

5

Harvesting Conversational Intelligence Using the Wisdom of Our Five Brains

I've learned that people will forget what you said, people will forget what you did, but people will never forget how you made them feel.

——MAYA ANGELOU

onversations are not just a way of sharing information (Level I); we have evolved over millions of years to a point where our conversations trigger physical and emotional changes in our brains and bodies. These changes may include the release of oxytocin, which fosters bonding and collaboration, but they may also include the release of cortisol, which is a "fear hormone," and testosterone, which boosts our more aggressive behaviors.

Many neuroscientists are working now on better understanding the neurotransmitters that are activated during conversation. At the Creating WE Institute, we have built an executive board that includes some of the world's most extraordinary scientists. Rex Jung PhD, Assistant Professor at the University of New Mexico, is our founding member who oversees the scientific board and advises us on applications to everyday life. Rex's specialty is creativity. Their work has informed this book, as has all of the research projects and consulting we do with our clients.

Another member of the executive board at the Creating WE Institute is Bruce S. McEwen, PhD, Alfred E. Mirsky professor and head of the Harold and Margaret Milliken Hatch Laboratory of Neuroendocrinology at Rockefeller University. McEwen believes:

> Trust is a phenomenon that is enhanced by oxytocin, which gets people to be socially interactive—to engage in conversations. That's only part of the story. Then you have the amygdala, located in the primitive brain, which is the sentinel, along with the prefrontal cortex (the more advanced brain), paying attention to decide if the interaction is going to be rewarding or punishing. They work as a team to help us know if we can trust being open or not trust and close down in our conversation. If the interaction is punishing or harshly threatening, we will feel more aggressive and distrustful. If we are unsure of the person's intentions, we will be wary and move into protect behaviors.

The role of the heart and our understanding of trust is a highly controversial subject in the field of neuroscience, yet it is becoming more clear as different neuroscientists share and compare what they are learning (Level III conversations) with one another. According to McEwen, "You have to master the hormonal and conversational 'balancing act.' This balancing act takes place in the brain, not the heart." McEwen believes that the brain orchestrates a conversation between the lower part of the brain (the primitive amygdala) and the higher brain centers such as the prefrontal cortex to communicate to other parts of the brain (the hypothalamus). This activates the release of hormones, such as cortisol, and stimulates the sympathetic and para sympathetic nerve pathways to the heart. McEwen gives master signaling to the brain.

Rollin McCrathy, PhD, and the research at the Institute of HeartMath discovered the critical link between emotions and heart rate variability (HRV) or heart rhythms. The heart responds to the hormones and beats either coherently or incoherently. Coherence in the heart, first introduced by Rollin McCrathy, PhD, results in a smoother heart rhythm that signals safety and trust, giving master signaling on the basis that there are more afferent nerves that go from the heart to the brain.

Along with McCrathy, PhD, Stephen Porges, PhD, who was known for his Polyvagal Theory, was the first researcher to identify heart rate variability, which links a coherent variability to trust and an incoherent variability to distrust. So we have an interesting symphony of approaches that neuroscientists use to translate the role of the heart in signaling "protection or partnering," "fear or trust," and "friend or foe." Heart rate variability plays a role in signaling both our fear networks and our trust networks. Our "heart brain" does more than pump blood throughout the body; it is connected to the brain through networks of afferent nerves that emanate from the heart itself. The heart communicates to the brain in so many ways—chemically, neurochemically, and energetically—which is why I believe it is part of the brain's regulatory system.

What we also know is that the amygdala is the region of the brain where fear and distrust reside, and the prefrontal cortex is where trust and growth reside. When the prefrontal cortex is not overwhelmed by fear hormones, it's able to exert a top-down control over the amygdala and limbic brain to quell fight, flight, and freeze reactions. So the heart works in concert with the other four brains to produce our human behavior.

The Brain's Landscape

What we now know is that the human brain has evolved over millions of years, and the older brain—what we call the reptilian brain and its sentinel, the amygdala—responds to physical and ego threats. When we are threatened, our listening changes and we listen with "threatened" ears. When we listen with threatened ears, we distort what we hear and selectively add fear-based interpretations and bad intent to what others are saying. Is the threat true? It is true to us, though it may not be true to the other person. Yet as we experience it, it becomes our truth.

Listening for Threats

The amygdala, the part of the reptilian brain that protects us from harm, is always listening for words and meanings that might threaten us. When it perceives threats—and it is the perception that matters—the amygdala releases chemicals designed to protect us from harm, and which activate the "flight or fight" reflex.

But those same chemicals prevent the thinking parts of our brain from playing a more active role—with the result that if you feel threatened, you are not going to have a productive meeting.

In fact, these chemicals direct our attention away from the conversation to inward thoughts that address our threat questions, which might include :

- Do I need to protect myself?
- Am I being included or excluded?
- Am I being appreciated and valued?

What we are learning is that the older brain is our default brain, and it responds to fear and distrust much more quickly than our newer brain can. Our newer brain enables growth, learning, and higher levels of connectivity with others, yet it takes more time to process what it knows or to make sense of what it believes. The brain works in concert with the higher brain centers to help us regulate our states of mind. This allows us to better connect with others, and when we connect we feel greater trust to open up and say what is on our minds.

Interestingly, because of the way our brains have evolved, the lower brain responds much more quickly. We read threats, or absence of them, first, and then our higher brain works to put words to our feelings. Some scientists assert that our lower brain responds at .07 seconds, while our higher brain, where language resides, operates at .1 second. Our brains have evolved to give us great ability to put words to what we feel and think, but our nonverbal processors carry greater weight in the meaning of what we experience and they make assessments at a much more rapid rate.

The nonverbal part of our conversations is much more important than the verbal element in defining the meaning of our interactions. Where feelings and emotions are involved, we can readily see the enormous value of understanding the impact and role of the older parts of the brain. Only when all the components of our mind–brain–body system work together in an integrated way can we fully trust others and ourselves. When we do, we can access our more strategic and advanced thinking skills.

Tapping Our Executive Intelligence

As we now know, the hormone oxytocin is a neurotransmitter associated with bonding behaviors. Paul Zak, PhD, from the Claremont Graduate University, senior author of the study "Trust Hormone Associated with Happiness," suggests that oxytocin could be the most prevalent hormone in the heart and the brain, and could be the critical driving force behind our need for social contact. Oxytocin, which is a peptide with nine amino acids, is produced within the brain, particularly in the pituitary gland and the hypothalamus, as well as in the ovaries and testes.

When oxytocin is produced, according to Zak, we feel happier, in addition to feeling more collaborative. This hormone's power is one of the more recent discoveries in neuroscience and may explain why, in its absence, isolation can be so painful, why loners die young, and why rejection is more painful at times than physical pain. Some scientists call oxytocin the "cuddle hormone" or "love hormone" because of its ability to make us feel cared for. Its power to create and restore a feeling of well-being is as good as a mother's hug.

OUR FIVE BRAINS

Behind the neuroscience of WE is a model for seeing our brains not as one brain but as five brains, each hardwired to help us sort out and sort through our interactions with others

- **The Reptilian Brain** informs us about threats (physical and psychological) to our safety (amygdala).

- **The Limbic Brain** helps us identify our friends and our foes and lets us know how to fit in; it is concerned with needs, emotions, and relationships.

- **The Neocortex** sorts through data from our senses, memories, and experiences, and helps us make sense of our reality— promotes understanding.

The other two brains work in concert, and influence what it means to be human:

- **The Heart Brain**, our oldest brain, reads the biochemistry of our bodies and enables us to translate the energetic and hormonal messages that arise as we interact.

- **The Prefrontal Cortex**, or **Executive Brain**, engages us with the outer world and the future, helping us grasp inner and outer truths. By translating current information, impulses, and biochemistry, it helps us make judgment calls, have empathy, and anticipate the future, what we call foresight.

Our brains are made to be social, so when we aren't paying attention to our own tasks and to-dos, we are connecting with others— that is what our brains need. Next time you are in a conversation, let the power of your five brains give you insight into how to respond.

FIGURE 5–1: Wisdom of the Five Brains

Heart Coherence

When we feel threatened, unappreciated, unfairly judged, bullied, or embarrassed, the heart brain responds to the perceived threat by beating faster. Blood rushes to the parts of our brain that need to be fired up to handle the perceived challenges. Rather than connecting to others, we move into "protect" behaviors. This fear response sends messages from the heart to other parts of the brain to stop connecting and start protecting.

When we are in *coherence*[1] with others (when we are in sync, connecting and bonding), on the other hand, our heart sustains a rhythm that communicates trust and signals our brains that it's safe to be open to influence. My Conversational Intelligence practices are built on the belief that Level III interaction dynamics are facilitated when we are in higher levels of coherence with others, and higher levels of coherence with others is facilitated by Level III conversations. This is a self-reinforcing system.

Neurotransmitters circulate in the brain and transmit signals from one nerve to another, amplifying the connectivity in the brain. Neurotransmitters are to the brain what conversations are to relationships. Each neurotransmitter has a function, and oxytocin has the function of creating "move toward others" behavior. It's a beautiful system that enhances overall integration of brain activity and signals our brains to allow others in. When we do so and we have a transformational experience with that person, we're immersed in a neurochemical bath of "happy hormones" that signal shared success with others. The communication that takes place at the chemical level far outweighs the communication that takes place at the verbal levels, as we'll see in the following discussion.

Our Bodies Do Most of Our Talking

However sophisticated an organization may be in its communications, our conversations with one another are far more complex than words on a printed page or the words that come out of our mouths. Communication through interaction is less about the words spoken than it is about the *interaction dynamics* that take place at the nonverbal level; it is at this level that trust is established—or not.

The importance of communication beyond mere words is not a recent discovery. In 1967 Albert Mehrabian isolated three elements that play a role when we convey feelings and attitudes to each other face to face. These are:

- Words
- Tone of voice
- Nonverbal behavior (such as facial expressions and eye contact)

In terms of importance, people allocate 7 percent to words, 38 percent to tone of voice, and 55 percent to nonverbal behaviors. For effective communication, these three aspects have to support one another. When they do not, people tend to assign the importance we see above—and nonverbal communication trumps words 100 percent of the time.

In the next few chapters we'll examine how to shape conversations so that we draw on the Wisdom of the Five Brains in the most effective ways. In spite of the complexity of the brain and the multilevel experience of interpreting our conversations with each other, our brains are designed for coherence. In fact, we listen better and speak better when we are in a state of trust and coherence with others and when all five brains are helping us interpret what is going on.

A fascinating discovery has come from the work of Professor Uri Hasson at Princeton University. Hasson explores the workings of the brain during interactions between people. His findings indicate that during successful communication, the speaker's and the listener's brains show the same patterns of activation. But when two people are both speaking in languages that the other doesn't understand (figuratively and literally), this "neural coupling" significantly diminishes.

Professor Hasson's work is opening a window on our understanding of the way brains synchronize their activity when we communicate effectively, giving us a new way of assessing both verbal and nonverbal signals. We are learning that rapport and trust are not givens. They are cultivated in environments where people practice having Level III conversations, in which aligning and connecting means honoring, respecting, and believing in others. Level III conversations foster trust much more than conversations in which the focus is on getting the facts right (Level I: informational, updating, and transacting basic business) or persuading another person (Level II: positional, influencing others to our point of view). Furthermore, the work of Hasson and other neuroscientists suggests that Co-creating Conversations have the power to literally rewire our brains. But I am getting ahead of myself. Let's start at the level where our social interactions have the greatest impact, the nonverbal level.

Harvesting Conversational Intelligence

Our brains function best when we are in trusting, healthy relationships. However, as we study the Wisdom of the Five Brains, we are learning that at times one of our brains is mastering the others. We can use the terms "master and slave" to explain how this process works.[2] When we are stressed and in fear, our reptilian brain becomes our master; when our expectations are not being met, our limbic brain steps in to provide us with information about how we feel and to give us guidance in navigating our journey with others—or against others (guiding us to determine whether they are friends or foes).

When we are figuring out how to handle situations, our neocortex becomes the *master* of our journey and gives us "scripts" for making sense of reality and taking action; when we need to focus on complex decisions, integrity and truth, and empathy and strategic thinking, our prefrontal cortex becomes our guide.

Heart–brain neuroscientific research teaches us that when our heart is in sync with other human beings, high levels of trust emerge. When our brain connects with others (when we are forming a deep relationship), we experience coherent heart patterns that send signals to the prefrontal cortex and the rest of the brain to trust and that we will not be harmed. We become open to others, we connect our views of reality, and we merge our best thinking to harvest new insights with others.

Human beings are the most highly social species on this planet. When we succeed in connecting deeply with others—heart to heart and head to head—trust is at its all-time high, and people work in concert in extraordinary ways. Social connection is what our brains need to do to be vital and healthy. Co-creating Conversations allow us to elevate our interaction dynamics to Level III, where we are transforming our ideas at the conscious level, and also shaping our DNA at the genetic level. Perhaps this sounds like science fiction, but it's not. Scientists are learning that our brain is more plastic and changeable than we ever imagined—our brains exhibit neuroplasticity.[3] In addition, we now know that while a percentage of our genes, called template genes, are not designed to change other genes, transcription genes are designed to be impacted by the environment. I believe that, through Co-creating Conversations and dynamic interactions with others, we engage and harvest this uniquely human, transformational capacity for shaping our DNA.

Another incredible facet to this story is that language is derived from a unique gene, the FOXP2 gene. Without this gene, we would not have language and could not carry on conversations. This gene is special. It is not the type of gene that gives us our hair color or our size and shape—as do template genes. The FOXP2 gene is a regulatory gene. It gives us language and, according to scientists, helps us regulate our emotions—either up-regulate (turn them higher) or down-regulate (lower) them. So conversations let us regulate our inner world of emotions and feelings. When we feel bad and someone consoles us, our cortisol is lowered and likely our oxytocin is elevated, making us feel trust and love, the same feelings we have when we are cared for. When we feel good and someone joins in our excitement, our endorphins increase and we feel better, we feel happier, we feel more connected.[4]

The Alchemy of Conversational Intelligence

What you are learning in this book is that conversations are not just a way of sharing information; they actually trigger physical and emotional changes in the brain that either open you up to having a healthy, trusting conversation or close you down so that you speak from fear, caution, and worry.

As we communicate, we trigger a neurochemical soup that makes us feel either good or bad, and we translate that inner experience into words, sentences, and stories. "Feel good" conversations trigger higher levels of dopamine, oxytocin, endorphins, and other chemicals that give us a sense of well-being.

When we converse with others, we are not only sharing information, we are sharing our inner world, or sense of reality. We are also validating reality with others. We are most importantly measuring the levels of trust in our relationship to determine whether we can share, open up, and partner with others—and the quality of our conversations depends on how open or how closed we feel at the moment of contact.

The millions of minute-by-minute neurochemical reactions within our brains drive our states of mind. These states of mind affect the way we build trusting relationships with others, how we communicate, and how we shape our relationships every day, all day long. Matt Lieberman and Naomi Eisenberger, scientists at UCLA, contend that our brains are designed to be social—and the need for human contact is greater than the need for safety. Eisenberger and Lieberman's research has shown that feeling socially excluded activates some of the same neural regions that are activated in response to physical pain, suggesting that social rejection may indeed be "painful."

Are Hugs Allowed at Work?

We have choices every day about how we influence each other.

For example, when a leader trusts that an employee will be able to tackle a project successfully, she communicates her confidence through subtle yet significant behavior. At this moment of contact something happens neurochemically between the leader and the employee—the two connect. And when they do, the uncertainty about whether the employee "belongs" disappears and the two move into a new mind-set of confidence in themselves and each other. They are able to experiment and take risks, they are able to learn and grow, and they are able to partner with others to handle the challenges of growing the business. I call the various ways a leader can show appreciation, support, or validation the Caring Effect; these behaviors trigger a more positive state of mind in the person on the receiving end of such support.

The Five Questions

When we connect with others, our mind toggles through a series of five hardwired questions at a pace so rapid our conscious mind doesn't know it's doing it. These questions and the answers we receive are subcognitive yet define the way our neurochemistry enables us to engage with others. The answers we receive determine whether we will open up and connect with others:

Question I: Protect How do I protect myself, and do I need to?
Question II: Connect Who loves me, who hates me, and can I trust this person?
Question III: Belong Where do I belong and fit in?
Question IV: Be strong What do I need to learn to be successful?
Question V: Partner How do I create value with others?

If a leader projects positive intentions and if the employee receives positive answers during the subliminal conversation he is having with the leader, the employee feels more confident in taking risks and accomplishing the task at hand. There is a neurochemical shift in the employee's confidence that can be directly connected to increases in neurotransmitters such as serotonin and dopamine. When this happens both people—employee and leader—are raising their conversational IQ.

When we receive public praise and support, we unlock yet another set of neurochemical patterns that cascade positive chemistry throughout the brain. Highly motivated employees describe the feeling of performing well as an almost drug-like state (because of the dopamine and endorphins released by these interactions, it is actually quite similar). When this state of positive arousal comes with appropriate, honest, and well-deserved (sincere) praise, employees feel they are trusted and supported by their boss. They will take more risks, speak up more, push back when they have things to say, and be more confident in their dealings with their peers.

6

Bringing Conversations to Life

The real voyage of discovery consists not in seeking new landscapes but in having new eyes.

—MARCEL PROUST

Too often, leaders become mired in one type of engagement, trying the same tactics again and again, hoping for different outcomes. I call getting stuck in Level I conversations the "Tell–Sell–Yell Syndrome."

Over my years working with leaders and teams, I've come to realize that people often have good intentions and think they are fostering great conversations when they are not. For example, a leader who realizes her team is not getting her message about the vision and mission of the company may "tell more," hoping that more information will make a difference. If telling more doesn't create the results she wants, the leader may "sell" her ideas to get people on board; when this doesn't work, she is inclined to "yell" to get results. Yet employees don't want more "vision," they want deeper engagement with leaders who can help them execute the vision. When those dynamics don't emerge, employees often go into protective behaviors, pulling back from engagement rather than stepping into it.

As an example of a leader who got caught up in the Tell–Sell–Yell

TELL-SELL-YELL SYNDROME

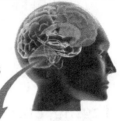

LEVEL I	LEVEL II	LEVEL III

Telling
Advice giving
Fixated on single strategy
Lacking interactive dynamics

Creates protect behaviors and loss of engagement.

FIGURE 6–1: Tell–Sell–Yell Syndrome

Syndrome, let's look at Jacques Nasser, who became CEO of Ford in 2000. Nasser's goal was to transform the company from a top-down, hierarchical organization to one that engaged the hearts and souls of its employees. In the beginning he was having great success. He set up town halls across the country and visited many locations, talking about how he wanted employees at all levels to have a voice and become engaged in helping the organization change. Yet when he didn't see the results of engagement come quickly enough, he became frustrated and started to voice his dissatisfaction. He went into Tell-Yell-Sell. His motivation turned to disappointment, and employees felt that shift. Soon the board stepped in and asked Nasser to step down as CEO. A powerful beginning transformed into a disappointing ending, as Nasser fell into the Tell–Sell–Yell Syndrome and didn't recognize its impact in time to do something about it. He fell back into Level I and Level II conversations without Level III engagement, a pattern ill-suited for the needs of a highly connected, changing marketplace.

When we look at stories of leaders who initially inspired engagement and then ultimately failed to move the organization forward, we find these same patterns repeating themselves.

Bob Lutz, on the other hand, a client of ours, now a retired vice chairman of General Motors, wanted to transform the global battery company Exide Technologies from a geographically based, location-centric company to a customer-centric company. Over a two-year period I worked with Bob to architect a process we aptly called "Recharging Exide," a global transformation and restructuring of the company that made it more customer-centric and innovative.

What made this engagement so powerful for me was a particular conversation I had with Bob; I asked him to decide the level of engagement he would be comfortable with as we moved forward with the transformation. As we sat together in his office I outlined the options: he could choose to structure the process using Level I conversations, in which case he'd send out e-mails and announcements describing the change, and expect that people will make it happen. He could even go and visit every one of the key locations globally and talk about the change, as Nasser did, believing he could engage each country's head and teams and persuade them to get on board with the change. He could do a top-down cascade of the new vision for Exide, and persuade everyone of the importance of the change, which would be exercising Level I (transactional and informational) and Level II (positional authority).

Bob chose instead to use a Level III transformational strategy and to engage the entirety of his worldwide organization in shaping and contributing to the transformation. Within eighteen months Exide transformed from a location-centric to a customer-centric organization, with the whole organization poised to work with customers in productive, innovative, and competitive ways.

Designed to Argue

Just as we can become stuck at Level I, we can get stuck at Level II. We often think that doing more of what we are already doing will yield better results, but it usually doesn't. In the case of Level II positional dynamics, we get neurochemically hooked on being right. This dynamic is about advocating and inquiring with the intention of influencing others to our point of view. Our brain likes to be right. When we are right, we get a dopamine hit, an addictive sensation. It feels great to be right, and our brain craves the positive emotions that come with it.

Hugo Mercier now at the Laboratoire Sur Le Langage, Le Cerveau Et La Cognition in Leon, and Dan Sperber at the Central European University in Budapest, Hungary, agree with the tenets of Conversational Intelligence in that, according to them, our brains have evolved to help us argue. An ability to argue convincingly would have been in our ancestors' interest as they evolved more advanced forms of communication.[1] At work, this behavior shows up in many meetings when we find a few leaders facing off on a subject of great importance to them. As they hit their stride in their persuasive power dance, they find it difficult to let go of winning, especially with their colleagues as spectators. So what may have started as an exchange of ideas can become a contest of wills, leaving one person the winner and the other the loser. Getting stuck in Level II results in becoming addicted to being right and failing to realize the negative impact this tendency has on others.

As with drugs, the feelings brought on by the flow of neurochemicals can lead to addictions. We can actually get addicted to being right. When we are right (and others are wrong), our brain produces feel-good hormones. Being right also makes us feel powerful, which can elevate testosterone and adrenaline—together these chemicals ramp up our ability to feel we are invincible and smarter than others. An addiction to being right causes many corporate cultures to become toxic. We see lots of "alpha dominance" and its corollary, people who are drummed into submission and lose their voice, then complain about it.

I often coach clients from large financial companies, insurance companies, and technology companies. The leaders are off-the-charts smart, and have been recognized as such by being promoted to C-level positions. With that type of reward comes the hidden yet profound belief that winning conversational battles will get them more. It often leads to the opposite, however; their style strikes others as argumentative and arrogant, and they appear willing to leave others in their wake. No one wants to feel stupid in front of peers (I call this tendency to walk over others the You Stupid Idiot, or YSI Syndrome). But having higher basic intelligence isn't the solution to making others feel worthy—cultivating Conversational Intelligence is.

Expanding What's Possible

Moving to Level III conversations allows us to release the power of true exchange with other human beings. As our Conversational Intelligence evolves, we become mindful of our conversational intention and notice the impact our conversations have on others. When we live in Level III conversations we realize that each of us brings our own meanings to the words we use. Our meanings and the way we link our ideas together are what make us each unique; and as we evolve our thinking, our words and what they mean evolve. Our understanding of meanings as created and co-created is critical to our recognition that a culture—whether of a country or a company—is the sum of co-created meanings. Every company has a culture, and its co-created meanings are unique to that culture. Deborah Ancona, a professor of Organization Studies at MIT, along with Peter Senge and other leadership experts, recognizes that "sense making" is one of the most important skills a new leader can possess.

In order to make sense of our reality, it is essential that we understand the value of *sharing and discovering*. Sharing and discovering is about harvesting new definitions based on our shared meanings and experiences. The right side of our Conversational Dashboard (see figure 6–2)—Level III conversation—is where we take into account our co-created reality:

- Meanings evolve
- We shape meanings with others
- We need to validate meanings with others
- Breakdowns occur when we hold different meanings than others

- Breakdowns occur when we try to persuade others our meanings are the right ones
- Breakthroughs occur when we take the time to share and discover
- Breakthroughs occur when we co-create and partner in creating a shared reality

Masters of Conversational Intelligence are able to recognize when they are on the same page with others and when they are not, and they can refocus, reframe, and redirect the conversation in ways that open the space for more discovery and dialogue. Some conversations may need to focus on unmet expectations or below-the-surface feelings of discontent, topics that often seem too difficult to address. Yet those who master Conversational Intelligence realize that Level III conversations are about opening the space for TRUST: Transparency, Relationship, Understanding, Shared success, Truth telling and testing assumptions. When we shape the space for TRUST, we keep the doors open for deeper exploration and discovery in order to harvest a picture of shared success. To do this we need to shift into a Level III mind-set: we must stay open and nonjudgmental, be willing to be influenced, and focus on listening with an open mind. It sounds easy but it's often challenging when we feel we may lose or when we feel threatened in subtle yet poignant ways.

In this chapter, I'll share a story that illustrates how to move from Level I to Level III through co-creating conversational rituals. We'll focus on how to give your conversations a makeover, one that will harvest great business results.

A Conversational Intelligence Makeover

It was not long ago that the very survival of the Clairol brand, now part of Procter & Gamble, was in doubt. Sales were falling dramatically.

Finger pointing was rampant. And not only were executives not on the same page, they were not even reading the same book.

Those in the Marketing Department thought that if they only created greater promotions business would turn around. Sales managers believed that greater incentives to the sales force would increase revenues, while those in the Advertising Department thought new commercials featuring younger consumers would turn things around.

What was apparent to me, as someone from outside the company, was that there was a clear lack of Conversational Intelligence, and my first job was to get inside and assess which side of the Conversational Dashboard characterized the current culture. My research surfaced what I imagined—they were operating out of Level I and Level II, yet trying to accomplish Level III challenges.

I discovered that people were simply not communicating in a way that created shared meaning about what needed to be accomplished and why. Executives in each department were coming up with ideas for how they might impact the company's bottom line, yet few were talking across the organization to figure out how they could get on the same page about how to face the market challenges with the level of certainty and courage characteristic of a company hoping to turn things around.

Think about the Conversational Dashboard. Organizations create transformation when they figure out how to move people forward from Level I or Level II, into Level III transformational conversations. I often introduce the Conversational Dashboard as a visual tool so teams can assess their levels of engagement, and when they do, they have a way of co-regulating the engagement to meet the needs of the situation. I use the Conversational Dashboard as a reminder and as a compass that helps direct the team to move conversations from transactional to transformational ones.

CONVERSATIONAL DASHBOARD™

FIGURE 6–2: Conversational Dashboard

What Does Level I Really Look Like?

Before we began our work on Conversational Intelligence at Clairol, the executive vice president in charge of Sales would stand up in front of the sales team and tell them what he wanted them to do: "We need to increase sales by 4 percent this quarter." Then he would tell them exactly how to do it: "I am handing out our new marketing scripts and I expect you to follow them to the letter." He was stuck on the far left of the dashboard in Level I dynamics, telling his team what to do. Sometimes he would venture into Level II, becoming strongly opinionated and advocating his position when resistance emerged. To move into Level III he needed to engage with the sales staff in "sharing and discovering" dynamics, which opened the space for his team to be included in the conversation, not just recipients of a dictum.

After he was coached toward a Level III conversational dynamic, this executive VP of Sales got up and shared the challenge that he and the rest of the organization faced. In his talk, he not only *asked* for help, he set the stage for a quantum leap into sharing, discovering, and co-creating: "We need to increase sales by 5 percent in this quarter to move us closer to our goal of dominating the category, that is: to become the category leader. I have some thoughts I would like to *share* with you, and I need your best thinking for the most effective way to accomplish this. How can we co-create this together?"

Orchestrating a Conversational Makeover

Conversation rituals are the heart of any transformational process. In fact, engaging conversational rituals are the catalyst that activates change without resistance and fear. As part of our Clairol Makeover, we constructed a safe space for transformation.

After coaching the senior executives on how to move from "Protect" to "Partner" and having them practice sharing, discovering, and co-creating, we moved on to creating the space for them to practice Conversational Intelligence across the organization. Let's talk through the steps of how Conversational Intelligence works in practice.

Each of the leaders knew that building and sustaining trust was an imperative. So they all operated from the TRUST Checklist, focusing on the intention of living in trust by:

✓ Being **Transparent**
✓ Focusing on building **Relationships**, respect, and rapport before focusing on the task
✓ Listening more deeply to **Understand** others' perspectives
✓ Focusing on **Shared success**, rather than only on self-interest
✓ **Truth telling and testing assumptions** about reality gaps when they existed to make sure they put them on the table to discuss

Once the leaders anchored and primed themselves for leading with trust, they were more open to new ideas and were able to facilitate better conversations, ensuring that their people were able to share, discover, and co-create around a vision of shared success.

Bringing Conversations to Life

When our work at Clairol began, the CEO, Steve Sadove, realized people were not on the same page. His key executives had different views on how to approach the company's business challenges—and their reality gaps were so big at times that conflicts about what to do dominated the executive suite. Sadove knew there needed to be full *transparency* about what was going on. He wanted to replace conflicts with *conversations.*

To create an environment in which people felt more open to co-creating, we built an internal news network. The Clairol News Network (which we quickly dubbed "CNN" internally) included *Visions,* a video news program, as well as two newsletters: *The Challenger,* which featured stories of people challenging the status quo, and *The Manager,* which focused on how to manage change. We used these vehicles to create one conversation across all of Clairol. Through these communication vehicles, all departments became part of one conversation in which everyone was positively influencing the Clairol Makeover, which, among other things, called for the company to update its image by offering natural hair color products rather than harsh, chemical dyes.

The Clairol News Network became a way to bring updates and success stories about the Clairol Makeover to all employees so that their fears of the company going out of business could be redirected into conversations that built teamwork and led to innovation.

Next, the company reorganized around the customer, creating teams with a customer-centric approach. New roles, responsibilities, and *relationships* were forged, and people made commitments to partner and share so that they could discover what the customer really needed. This commitment to the customer allowed team members with disparate interpretations about which priorities were most important to refocus around customers and to put the customers' benefit at the center of all decisions and actions.

For example, each customer-centric team had five or six people, with members representing one of the key business functions—Sales, Marketing, Promotions, etc.—that needed to work together. In addition, the Sales team met with the Research and Development (R&D) team regularly to *share feedback* and insights from customers so that new product development was based on ongoing customer feedback.

Each customer-centric team stepped into another's shoes to *understand* reality from the other's perspectives. In doing so, the teams learned more about how each could help the other and, most importantly, the customer. This revolutionized the way Clairol created products, the way the Marketing Department worked with Promotions, the way Sales worked with innovation teams, and so on.

As part of the program, we created a vision of *shared success*—with becoming the category leader the overarching goal—and we talked about it over and over again through the *Visions* video news network. To sustain the highest levels of sharing, discovering, partnering, and co-creating, we interviewed executives, researchers, sales and marketing executives, and financial executives about the Clairol Makeover. My role as the producer of the program was to make sure the discussions and exchanges operated at the highest level of Conversational Intelligence.

My provocative interviews got people thinking together about what it meant to be a category leader and sparked conversations about what role each could play in making this goal a reality. In other words, everyone worked together on *telling the truth* and closing the reality gaps. Over the course of the project we distributed the *Visions* videos throughout the company, ensuring that everyone's view of success was aligned. In addition to the videos, the *Manager* and *Challenger* publications were distributed to employees to reinforce the company's new direction and also to give people a tool for expanding the conversations at all levels of the organization, making sure that everyone understood what category leadership was and how to get there.

We used the Clairol News Network to broadcast updates about progress, reinforce key milestones, and share stories and successes. Using the principles we talked about earlier—Transparency, Relationship, Understanding, Shared success, Truth telling and testing assumptions—we taught senior executives how to run town hall meetings in a way that would draw out perspectives from the field. We wanted to engage everyone in shaping the future of the company. We wanted to make sure the leaders were now facilitators of Conversational Intelligence.

As a result of this intensive Conversational Makeover, Clairol employees began seeing success with the same eyes: they were *telling each other the truth* about what was working and what was not and were *sharing and discovering* in order to bridge reality gaps. Whether employees were part of an innovation team or were creating new product formulas or promotions, everyone was part of the same conversation and all were aligned on what success looked like and how to achieve it together.

With the levels of adrenaline and cortisol decreasing and the levels of oxytocin rising, people found it easier to work together, and trust began to form organization-wide. This newfound spirit of collaboration allowed Clairol's management to not only transform the company, but also the industry.

The biggest shift at Clairol was the move from "telling–asking" (Level I) as the primary conversational dynamic to a "sharing–discovering" (Level III) style of interaction. People began to ask questions for which they had no answers. They were open to influence, inspired to innovate, and motivated to stay engaged even during difficult conversations. The organization grew from $250 million to $4.5 billion in less than a decade.

Clairol became the recognized leader in hair care and hair color (note, not hair dye). If you go into any large drug store or mass market retailer today you will see hair color products of all types, including products from different companies, sitting inside the Clairol Color Choice System, twenty-one linear feet of product, information, and advice, proof of the company's category leadership. In 2001, P&G bought the once-struggling company for $4.95 billion.

As Clairol executives learned, the right conversations done the right way can turn a dying company into full color! Through Conversational Intelligence, we learn to work with others to describe the present and see, shape, and predict the future, building a bridge between where we are and where we would like to be.

7

Priming for Level III Conversations

Your vision will become clear only when you look into your heart. . . Who looks outside, dreams. Who looks inside, awakens.

—CARL JUNG

Imagine that you had hardwired instincts that gave you the ability to immediately—in a nanosecond—read another person's intentions. That is, to determine whether the person is trustworthy or not. And based on your gut instincts, your brain knew to either open up or close down, to share or to withhold. Well, you do! We all do.

What I've learned over the years is that the best communicators learn to align their intentions with their impact. While intention is what someone wants to make happen or plans to accomplish, the impact involves the quality of the experience from the perspective of the receiver—and that impact may not correspond with what the communicator intended. When communicators monitor and align intention and impact successfully, people trust them more fully. Once we move within ten feet of another human being, we come into contact with each other's energy fields, and are able to read how much we are able to trust the other person.

It's my thesis that this exquisite meter exists in all of us, and I often refer to these amazing human skills as our **Vital Instincts.** I believe our Vital Instincts are hardwired into our sensory system, letting us pick up cues about others' trustworthiness. These instincts provide us with an invisible checklist that we use to determine who is foe and who is friend. And because the instincts are so visceral, they reside in our primitive brain, which responds faster than all the other parts of our brain.

In the Vital Instincts Chart, consider each question a biological screening process. When we feel people are fair, honor our ownership, show reciprocity, are cooperative, allow us to have a voice, and honor our status in the tribe, we feel we can trust them. If not, we feel we need to be cautious and distrust them.

Think about your relationship with people at work. Identify someone you feel you can trust. See if you can check off each of these dynamics in your relationship with that person.

VITAL INSTINCTS™—FORCES THAT IMPACT TRUST:
FAIRNESS **O**WNERSHIP **R**ECIPROCITY **C**OOPERATION **E**XPRESSION **S**TATUS

FIGURE 7–1: Vital Instincts: FORCES

- Fairness: Does this interaction and relationship feel fair—are we establishing a "WE" or is this relationship about "I"? Are we sharing in the "food for thought"?
- Ownership: Do we have a sense of ownership—a stake in the ground—and is it clear what is mine and what is yours? Do we have rules of engagement regarding ownership?
- Reciprocity: Do I care for you and you for me? What are the positive actions we take on each other's behalf?
- Cooperation: In what ways do we join forces and work to support each other in achieving our needs?
- Expression: Do we give each other room to speak up and share what's on our minds? Do we give each other space to speak our thoughts?

- Status: Do we honor where we stand in the social hierarchy, and do we respect each other for where we stand?

Sensing Another's Presence at the Speed of Light

If it is true that human beings sense friend or foe in .07 seconds, it means we can tell whether we can trust a person just by the way he moves. The amygdala is hardwired to do this so we can protect ourselves from harm. When we look at it this way, it's not difficult to see how remarkable our human communication system really is. We not only focus on the tasks at hand, our brains simultaneously assess *how much we can trust others* to deliver on the tasks at hand.

Despite the complexity of this system, when we communicate with others we essentially either feel good or feel bad. We feel good when we have a sense of fairness, ownership, reciprocity, cooperation, open expression, and status. This state coexists with neurotransmitters such as dopamine and serotonin (the happy neurotransmitters), as well as oxytocin (a bonding hormone); together these neurotransmitters buffer against stress and produce pleasure. When we consistently feel good around certain people, that feeling typically leads to greater trust. And when we feel trust, the cycle is reinforced. Trust leads to rewards that go beyond words and feelings: they are a neurochemical reality.

On the other hand, when we communicate with others in ways that makes us fearful, sad, depressed, upset, angry, or overly stimulated, our fear chemistry is roused and we experience excess supplies of dopamine. This over stimulates the sympathetic system (flight or fight); increases levels of norepinephrine (stress hormone), which alerts us to threats; increases testosterone, which spurs aggression; and cascading levels of steroids, which enhance physical strength. When we are threatened, agitated, angered, or moved to fight, these chemicals are asserting themselves in the body. It's no wonder that we are distrustful of people when we feel they are rejecting us —both at a cellular level and a cognitive level, we decide that *another person doesn't have our best interest at heart*—and whether that impression is true or not, we create a story that casts our relationship in a negative or uncertain light.

Fortunately or unfortunately, when our fear and distrust of others is triggered, the neurochemistry associated with those feelings has a much longer-lasting effect than when our trust chemistry is activated. Scientists say that when cortisol, the fear hormone, is released, it has a twenty-six-hour shelf life in the body. If we continue to ruminate about an experience and trigger more fear, we can extend our sense of ill-ease for days, months, or even years. This is why leaders need to understand how to shape conversational environments for trust. Productivity, collaboration, creativity, and good business results all depend on it. We can't get to Level III conversations without understanding how to handle the interaction dynamics of conversations—and to do that we need to develop the Third Eye.

Getting in Front of the Curve

There are ways we can develop our ability to align our intentions with their impact. This is what Conversational Intelligence is all about. We need to become masters at observing our inner word of desires and observing the impact our actions have on others. The more these are aligned, the more we elevate our trust quotient, the trust placed in us by others.

Using Our Third Eye

When conversations trigger the primitive brain, we lose our executive functions. That means that the part of our brain that contains our ability to connect, empathize, judge courses of action, and come up with fresh ways of engaging with others is disconnected from our conversational ability. We no longer have access to that part of the brain, so we rely on the part that is active—our "fight, flight, freeze, or appease" impulses.

THE THIRD EYE

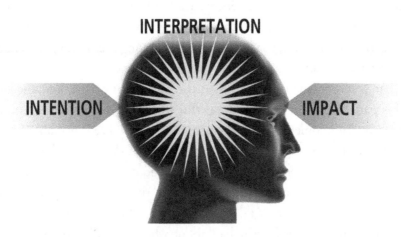

FIGURE 7–2: The Third Eye

When all goes well in a conversation, we have an intention to communicate and we connect. The impact is positive, which enriches both parties. In addition to being positive, when we are communicating from Level III dynamics, we are more honest and candid about our communication, and we are more vulnerable and open to sharing. That is why we call Level III the "share and discover" dynamic. At Level III, we are feeling so much trust with others that we are able to open up and share what is on our minds at the deepest level, and we can explore and discover what's on others' minds without judgment.

When, instead of triggering a state of trust, a conversation creates a sense of threat, and stimulates the primitive brain, we converse from that limited reservoir of skills. To make matters worse, we make stuff up—make our own interpretations—about what's going on and we disconnect from others even more.

The antidote for falling into permanent disconnection and distrust is to activate your Third Eye. When I work with leaders, I ask them to envision an eye in the middle of their forehead. This eye is where wisdom resides. This part of our forehead is where the executive brain also lives. My intention is to engage leaders in activating their prefrontal cortex, the part of the brain that can reflect on what is happening from a neutral point of view, see other ways of viewing a situation, and choose alternatives that will serve their relationship better.

As you've learned, trust lives in the prefrontal cortex, and engaging this part of our brain neutralizes threats and allows us to see alternatives in the moment, alternatives that have not been available before. Leaders who only focus on their intention, and do not see their impact, are living in an I-centric world. Leaders who develop a Third Eye bring intention and impact together and adjust the conversation to create a more positive impact. You may be saying, "What if my intention is to make someone feel really bad about what he did?" I'm going to ask you, as your coach, "Why would you want to do that?" If the answer is "It will make me feel better," then you are probably living in Level I or II when you answer. This is a starting place for coaching you into Level III.

Level III is a mind-set of partnering and co-creating; when you are living as an open, trusting, engaging, honest, candid, and caring person. You are also open to influence and willing to entertain new thoughts, even if you don't know how to act on them right way. You are open to being compassionate and to listening nonjudgmentally, and you are able to share with others your vulnerabilies and uncertainties. You are willing to be a human being, with your heart engaged, because you trust the other person to be willing to stay in this incredibly open space with you—or to let you know when she cannot.

Becoming consciously aware of your state of mind is critical to developing your Conversational Intelligence. Ask yourself, What impact are my words having on others? Is my thinking I-centric or WE-centric? These different approaches—and different states of mind—have dramatically diffferent impacts on the conversations you have and the outcomes you create. When you are perceiving with your Third Eye, you are able to step back and ask yourself if you are triggering your territorial instincts (distrust/protect) or your vital instincts (trust/growth). Once you recognize the difference, you can gain mastery over your mind-set, link intentions with impact, and create healthy work environments through healthy conversations.

Priming the Pump!

There is a way to get in front of the curve and reduce the threats and fears that turn on the reptilian brain and keep us stuck in protective behavior. The technique is called priming.

What is priming? Priming is the implicit effect that takes place when exposure to a stimulus influences the subsequent response. It can occur following perceptual, semantic, or conceptual stimulus repetition.

It happens, for example, if a person reads a list of words including the word "table" and is later asked to complete a word starting with the letters "tab." The probability that the person will answer "table" is greater than if she is not so primed. Another example is when people see an incomplete sketch that they are unable to identify: they are shown more of the sketch until they recognize the picture. Later, they will identify the sketch at an earlier stage than was possible for them the first time.

Priming causes us to think in a different way and changes our mind about how we will approach a task. In a business setting, priming lets us think about what we want to create—to design the conversational space—and allows the interaction dynamics to be flooded with the positive neurotransmitters that foster high levels of positive engagement. Priming helps us set the stage to achieve great results with others.

The effects of priming can be very salient and long lasting, even more so than simple recognition memory in the examples above. Priming can have an unconscious impact on events, on relationships, on trust building, and on the trajectory of our conversations. Even factors like physical environment can prime us to have certain perceptions. Believe it or not, the temperature of the coffee we drink at work can increase trust.

In 2007, when I first contacted John Bargh at Yale University, he was in the throes of conducting and interpreting his studies on hot and cold coffee. I was blown away with the results and the implications of the results!

Psychologists have long noted the importance of warm physical contact between caregivers and children in the children's ability to develop healthy relationships as adults, so Bargh and his research partner, Lawrence E. Williams, decided to test the impact of warmth on the perceptions of adults. To test their hypothesis about the importance of temperature, the research team casually asked that the undergraduate test subjects briefly hold either a warm cup of coffee or iced coffee as they wrote down information.

The subjects were then given a packet of information about an individual and asked to assess his or her personality traits. The participants assessed the person as significantly "warmer" if they had previously held the warm cup of coffee rather than the iced coffee. On personality scales unrelated to the trait of "warmth," the researchers found no difference in the way participants who held iced, versus hot, coffee responded.

In the second study, participants held heated or frozen therapeutic packs as part of a product evaluation study and were then told they could receive a gift certificate for a friend or a gift for themselves. Those who held the hot pack were more likely to ask for the gift certificate for a friend, while those who held the frozen pack tended to keep the gift.

"It appears that the effect of physical temperature is not just on how we see others, it affects our own behavior as well," Bargh said. "Physical warmth can make us see others as warmer people, but also causes us to be warmer—more generous and trusting—as well."

This demonstration of the power of temperature on character assessment has been supported by recent brain imaging studies. For instance, the experience of hot or cold stimuli has been shown to trigger strong activity in the insular cortex which is linked to emotion and cognitive function as well as interpersonal experiences. Researchers have also implicated the same area of the brain in borderline personality disorder, a debilitating illness characterized by an inability to cooperate and a near-complete inability to determine whom to trust.

Have you ever thought of your conversations like hot and cold coffee? When you talk with someone, are you creating a sense of cold and pushing the person away, or are you envisioning a sense of warmth and pulling him toward you? Neuroscientists have discovered something really fascinating. It turns out that a physical sensation of coldness and the feeling that a person is behaving coldly toward you are registered in the same place in the brain. Therefore, the brain reads environmental cues, equating rejection and cold, while also equating appreciation and warmth. Hence the common term "cold shoulder" to represent rejection. Without realizing it, we can bring warm and cold feelings into conversations and influence how people feel toward us—we can influence how trustworthy they find us and how approachable we are at the moment of contact. Priming can change the direction and trajectory of a conversation by turning a potentially cold conversation into a warm one.

Putting Priming into Action

How can you prime important conversations in your life? One thing you can do is change the environment or physical space to make it more favorable to conversation. This means changing the *context* surrounding a conversation so it feels warm rather than cold. For example, where people sit at a table can influence conversation: a person sitting at the head of a table brings into play a dynamic of authority (cold) over the others, while people gathered around a round table promotes a feeling of warmth.

It's also helpful to know how you can prime a person for an important conversation. Building rapport with a person before you begin a difficult conversation increases his trust in you; his feeling about you before the conversation will have an impact on how he interprets what you say. Our brain equates cold with caution, and caution triggers the lower brain to feel distrust. How can you learn to identify distrust in an environment and quell fears and uncertainty so your conversations begin on a warmer, more trusting note? How can you learn to recognize when you are in a state of fear, uncertainty, and apprehension, and prime yourself? How can you see in advance the impact you are having on your conversations, relationships, teams, and organization?

To begin, do a quick self-awareness check:

- Are you withdrawing and excluding others?
- Are you defensive and reactive, setting the context for territorialism to emerge?
- How can you shift your mind-set from exclusion to inclusion and set a new context for open, trusting conversations that enable you and others to partner for mutual success?

Warm or Cold? The Choice Is Yours

In preparation for important meetings, relationships, encounters, team sessions, or any time you want to create a positive context for your interactions with others, there are things you can to do to prime your brain for the best outcomes. Think of priming as a way of preparing the soil so you can establish a healthy garden.

As we discussed earlier, John Bargh discovered in his study on the effects of hot and cold coffee that simply holding one or the other before having a conversation actually triggers different parts of the brain to light up. Warm coffee signals warm encounters and cold coffee signals cold encounters. Bargh also did experiments with hard and soft chairs, with similar results—soft chairs made conversations easier and hard chairs made them stiffer. You may think this is a bunch of hogwash, but the effects of environment are real. In the business world, there are applications of this wisdom that may surprise you.

For more than a decade I've been working with a large global professional services firm as one of fourteen executive coaches. In one of the exercises we do with each group of fifty partners, we give them a list of seven adjectives that describe a fictitious person. We then ask the executives to make judgment calls about what these people would be like. Half the partners get seven words with the word "cold" in the middle of the list, and the other half get the word "warm." Then we watch hands going up as we call out the question—is this person more likely to be trusted or distrusted?

What astounds the room is that "cold" and "warm" are the only words on the two lists that are different, yet in almost every case, those with the word "cold" on their list assess the person as not to be trusted, while those with the word "warm" on their list of adjectives assess the person as trustworthy. Given this research and the insights we've discovered, there are things you can do, not to *manipulate*, but to *prime* your conversations for the best outcomes.

Because intention matters, priming must be done with the goal of sincerity and honesty. It must be done with mindfulness for true partnering and not as an act of deception or as a power play. Our minds and hearts pick up deception and manipulation before anything else—remember, we're hardwired to protect ourselves.

Priming Before

There are a number of actions you can take before your conversations even begin to create a context for success. There are practices you can adopt at work to trigger bonding, trust, and understanding. When you are with people with whom you have low levels of trust, you can raise the level of trust neurochemically by shaking hands. When you reach out to shake hands, oxytocin is released, which triggers the brain to react: "This is a friend, not a foe."

Now, it may take a few times before this feeling locks in fully, but each handshake improves your trust levels. Oxytocin release is like a chemical cocktail in the brain that shifts our perception of people. *It removes uncertainty.* We may say to ourselves, "Well, he's not so bad after all," and may not even know why we think this. Shaking hands before a negotiation increases the chance of a positive outcome.

Rules of Engagement

You can shift the outcome of a meeting by starting with a trust-building activity. This signals the amygdala to slow down and be quiet, and allows other parts of the brain to actively seek data that says this will be a good, trusting experience. The best way to set up a meeting for increased trust is to start by establishing rules of engagement.

Rules of Engagement Exercise

One way to do this exercise is to work with a flip chart in the front of the room, with "Rules of Engagement" written at the top of the page. Ask everyone in the room to identify the practices, or "rules," that would give this conversation and meeting the best outcome. Most people will express some variation of, "We will have an open, trusting conversation and will follow through on our agreements." In fact, stating that as one of the basic rules is a great idea. Then ask people to identify the conditions —behaviors, attitudes, and the like—necessary to create the most trusting conversational space.

As people add to the Rules of Engagement, their brain chemistry changes. Their amygdala feels satisfied that it doesn't need to act as the "protector," and the conversation settles down. The limbic brain—our emotional vault—is being taken care of because people are talking about the conditions under which real emotions can be shared safely (for example, one rule might be: "We will all listen to each other without judgment"). The neocortex is invited to participate when we make rules such as "Every idea is valuable." The prefrontal cortex is open and ready to think empathetically, because once the amygdala is quieted, neurochemical messages sent to the prefrontal cortex let it know it's safe to operate.

What this means is that trust will increase in individual relationships and among teams and organizations when we create the conversational conditions for reduced amygdala stimulation—which elicits fear and protective impulses—and more prefrontal cortex and heart brain connection.

Shaping the Space for Trust and Openness

At meetings, many of our clients sit at the head of the table, while their counterparts sit at the other end. When people assert positional authority in this way they send "alpha dominant" signals to the brain. By sitting in oppositional locations, they claim positional power rather than signaling that they are there to partner. To moderate this power stance and send signals of trust to your counterpart, you can do several things in advance of a meeting :

- **Send the agenda ahead of time:** Be open to suggestions for adding agenda items.
- **Expand the circle of trust:** Ask who else might attend the meeting and who would benefit from being included in the conversation.
- **Send a revised agenda:** Resend the agenda with the new items added from attending parties who submitted them.
- **Rethink seating:** At the meeting, sit with your counterpart, not in an oppositional seat. Put the agenda in front of both of you and work on it together—write on it and capture ideas on it together.
- **Attend to the quality of the conversation:** As a result of the preceding steps, the tenor of the meeting will change. Focus on keeping conversations open, collaborative, and non-oppositional.

These space-shifting actions really make a difference in the way conversations unfold. Our brains sense when space is shrinking and when it's expanding. Expanding is read as "growth" while shrinking space is interpreted as limiting autonomy and growth. These actions are concrete signals that tell our brains how to act and react to the person who has both expanded us and made us feel bigger, or limited us and made us feel smaller.

Priming During

Once we're enmeshed in a "cold" attitude, how do we return to "warm" feelings? The secret is to disengage and reengage. During meetings and in conversations we can find ourselves in awkward moments. We may disagree with someone, face a conflict, or hit a brick wall. We can see it coming—there will be a collision. We know things might get worse, and this may send us into an emotional state in which we're not open to listening anymore, or where we get more entrenched in our own point of view with every word.

When this is about to happen, the best negotiators use a technique called "disengaging." Disengaging allows you to tactfully stop the meeting and take a break, so that you can come down from your "Ladder of Conclusions" and let go of some of the emotions that may be blocking good judgment. When we are at the top of the ladder, we have our minds made up, we see the world only from our perspective, and we stop listening to others. Disengagement is a healthy negotiation tactic that can improve the conversation and that also quells the amygdala and other fear centers. This practice down-regulates cortisol and arousal neurotransmitters so they have less impact on your system and on the conversations. With reduced cortisol, your ability to tap into your higher brain powers is restored; your willingness to look for common ground will return, and the chances for a better resolution will emerge.

Research on negotiation has shown that when people disengage during a difficult negotiation with the intention of coming back to the discussion with a new and better strategy, they are more successful. The break serves to give people a chance to open their mental space and think of new and more productive ways to get a win–win. Strange as it may seem, when we step away from a difficult situation and take a break, we are interrupting a negative mental pattern, and the opportunity to think more broadly emerges. To create this moment during a negotiation you can:

- Suggest a "rest" or "vacation" from the conversation for a specific time frame.
- Use humor to disengage in the moment (this can also have a powerful priming impact); this strategy only works if this type of humor comes naturally to you.

Knowing When You Are Raising Your C-IQ

Use the Conversational Dashboard as a visual reminder for how to shape the conversational space. Our engagement with others makes us feel either that we need to protect ourselves or that we want to partner. When we feel we need to protect ourselves, we withdraw, become defensive, or attack. When we are in this I-centric, protective mode, we no longer think about protecting our brand or our team, we think about protecting ourselves, turning to reactive behaviors aimed at avoiding being hurt. With this attitude, we abdicate our leadership, separate ourselves from our employees, and create a true leadership vacuum. As a result, our conversations are less engaging, truthful, and trusting. WE-centric leadership, on the other hand, brings us closer to others, enabling us to see the truth, tackle tough issues head on, and build a mutually shared view of reality.

As you learn to use the Conversational Dashboard as a mental framework, you will become more conversationally agile and your

Conversational Intelligence will increase. This framework will give you a tool for gauging where you are and where you need to move to elevate the levels of engagement in yourself, your team, and your organization.

Co-Regulating the Conversational Space

Not every situation requires Level III dynamics. However, there are many difficult conversations that we shy away from because we are caught in Level II positional dyanmics and we become triggered by power-over-others issues that drive us to lower levels. By developing our Third Eye, and by staying in an open mind-set in which we "share and discover," we can sustain rapport, invite higher levels of innovation, and cultivate better, more productive relationships even with people who might have, in the past, felt like foes.

By using conversational tools to create a safe conversational space and by using the Conversational Dashboard, you and your colleagues become co-regulators of your emotional experience. In the way that emotional intelligence focuses on self-regulation, Conversational Intelligence focus on *co-regulation*, one of the most powerful tools for leaders, teams, and organizations to learn for success in the twenty-first century.

8

Conversational Agility:
Reframing, Refocusing, Redirecting

Change is the law of life. And those who look only to the past or present are certain to miss the future.

—JOHN F. KENNEDY

As you develop your conversational awareness, begin to "see" with your Third Eye, and get in front of potential conversational collisions, you will start to recognize when you need to change your navigational pattern during a conversation.

Reducing Fear

In a study examining healthy self-regulation, there was a 23 percent reduction in cortisol and a 100 percent increase in DHEA (a steroid hormone made by the adrenal glands) with intentional practice of regulating negative thought loops. This means that stress was dramatically reduced and well-being increased through mindful practices, breathing techniques, and heart appreciation.[1]

Enhancing Conversational Agility

Conversational Intelligence calls upon awareness from the listener as well as from the speaker—listening awareness must be even greater if the person is a leader. The reason we're listening determines the type of information we listen for. For example, salespeople listen for customer concerns and lawyers listen for the opposing speaker's faulty logic.

Each professional is trying to guide someone from point A to point B. The salesperson wants to move a customer from a point of interest to a point of sale. To navigate from point A to point B, leaders can employ the dashboard, or framework for listening, which includes asking the right questions and then, importantly, listening carefully to the employee's answers—to phrasing, context, and words—to get the real meanings behind the words.

The Value of Dashboards

Visual Dashboards are the next generation of leadership communication tools for building alignment and tracking outcomes. Dashboards create a shared visual and relational framework that enables people to "see" complex relationships in a simple way. Dashboards can be invisible or visible, and both can be used to gauge the health of an organization's conversations and improve them by applying Conversational Intelligence.

Invisible Dashboards

An invisible dashboard is one that is hardwired into our DNA. It's instinctual, subconscious, and intuitive. Becoming aware of how our vital instincts are hardwired and how our bodies gauge the trustworthiness of a person even before we get deep into a conversation is an example of our hardwired invisible dashboard. As you learned in the previous chapter, when you interact with another person you are keeping track of his level of Fairness, Ownership, Reciprocity, Cooperation, Expression, and Status, monitoring what it will like be to partner with the person and how open he is to both giving and receiving information. Based on these internal measures, you build expectations about how trustworthy others may be—or how much you can trust them to come through for you.

We all know that we trust those who care about us and are fair, are clear on ownership of tasks and responsibilities, reciprocate, cooperate, give us space and time to express what's on our mind, and value our contributions. We distrust those who do not play by these rules. These dashboards are turned on at all times, whether we're aware of them or not. But by tapping into our Conversational Intelligence, leaders can turn the invisible into the visible.

Visible Conversational Dashboards

LEVEL SETTING

VISIBLE CONVERSATIONAL DASHBOARDS CAN HELP US
MOVE FROM ONE LEVEL TO ANOTHER

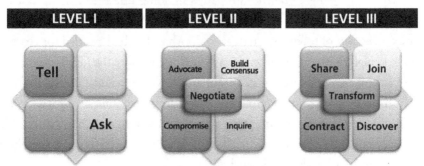

FIGURE 8–1: Level Setting

The purpose of creating visible conversational dashboards is to give us a visual language to know when we are in Level I, II, or III conversations and when we are "stuck" in any or all of them. Visual dashboards like the Conversational Dashboard offer a way for us to gain alignment about "where we stand with others," which is a key question for each person within a conversation. We have to ask, as Tom Cruise did in the movie *Knight and Day*, "With me…without me…with me…without me…" Through Conversational Dashboards, we are able to put words to the feelings we have about others being unfair with us, or taking advantage of us, or taking up too much airtime—all the exchanges that make us worried about how much we can trust others. In a larger sense, dashboards help us identify gaps where conversations can help bring reality more in line with expectations, increasing our chances to partner with others in a healthy and innovative way.

Teaching Conversational Agility

Conversational Dashboards became a reality for me a decade ago when I was called in to work with New Wave Entertainment (NWE) a high-profile entertainment company in Hollywood. The company culture was rife with destructive politics, the owners were not in sync, and distrust characterized the company's way of life. Over the course of several months, I assessed the company's leaders, diagnosed the nature of their challenges, and saw that distrust was going to be the company's undoing unless leadership put the real issues on the table. The company's directors decided to take twenty-five executives out of town for a retreat to do what they had avoided for years—talk straight with one another. I was asked to facilitate the meeting.

As the first morning session got underway, I could practically taste the fear in the room. People were avoiding eye contact and were sitting as far away as possible from those with whom they had issues. The steady buzz of nervous small talk reminded me of the first day of school after summer break—awkward and tense.

As I stood quietly at the front of the room, an idea came to me that would turn out to be the game changer—both for them and for me.

THE ARC OF ENGAGEMENT™

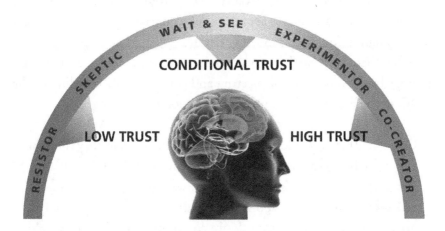

FIGURE 8–2: The ARC of Engagement

On a large flipchart I drew an arc. At the far left of the arc I wrote "Resistor," then "Skeptic," followed by "Wait-and-see" in the middle; to the right I wrote "Experimentor," and to the far right "Co-creator." After giving my graphic a name—The ARC of Engagement (The Gauge)—I turned to the gathered executives and said, "I'd like you each to identify where you are on this gauge." As the silence stretched on, I found myself tensing up. What if they didn't take up my challenge? Then I heard a voice in the back say, "I'm sitting in 'skeptical'; I don't believe that we're going to make any headway over the next few days."

My butterflies disappeared as people began to speak about how they were feeling, with a level of openness I had not seen from the group before. After two days, the leadership team had generated numerous powerful insights into the company's troubles as well as ideas about how to transform their culture. Over the next few years, this moderately successful entertainment company became the darling of Hollywood studios. Its business took a quantum leap forward, and within a few years the company's revenues increased more than twentyfold. More importantly, it now had a reputation as a great place to work, and was attracting new talent. Every executive who attended that first weekend retreat remembers it as the beginning of a journey into trust that laid the foundation for success moving forward.

After that weekend I interviewed the attendees and captured their feelings both going into the meeting and coming out. According to the COO of the organization, one response stood out:

> Going in, there was a lot of trepidation. Someone said they thought they were being sent away to a "growth camp." I think people were afraid that if they didn't "grow," they were going to be fired. No one was given a choice about participating, which was probably a good thing. If we had been told we could opt out, everyone would have. The real fear was that if we participated and somehow failed, we would be out of a job.
>
> Before that weekend I used to compare us to a submarine, all submerged. But today we can have discussions about things we would never discuss before. We talk about performing and not performing; we discuss conflicts that occur. We get through the discussions with honest communication. Our business has transformed itself.

By using the Conversational Dashboard tool, the executives learned to see where people were in the conversation—"Protect and Primitive Brain" or "Partner and Executive Brain." This experience brought with it great insights; as the executives learned to map the interaction dynamics taking place in the room, they could see what types of interactions disabled conversations and what types enabled healthy conversations. Once they understood how to have productive conversations, the team took control of their destiny.

In addition to using Conversational Dashboards to see where people are in a conversation, teams can also learn to reframe, refocus, and redirect their conversations to move them from a protective or positional stance, to a partnering one. These "three Rs" can help you interrupt a conversational pattern that is not working and let you access Level III wisdom in the moment, even in the face of conflict or the negative power of emotional triggers.

Navigating to New Places

To begin, let's imagine that you are starting to use Conversational Dashboards in your meetings and interactions with colleagues to determine everyone's frame of mind. Let's say you find that people are generally Resistors or Skeptics, and are in a closed state of mind. When this occurs, you will want to ask them a discovery question like, "What would it take for you to feel more engaged, or to want to co-create?" Asking discovery questions is a profoundly important yet simple way of getting people to move toward more co-creative ways of engaging in conversations. There are times, however, when this may not work, and you may need to transform the conversational space so you and others can move forward together. This is when you draw upon transformative conversational skills such as reframing, refocusing, and redirecting.

Reframing

Reframing is a miraculous conversational tool for taking a difficult situation and turning it into an opportunity for finding trust and *common ground* with someone. Even the phrase "common ground" is provocative and powerful. We are learning that conversations have space, and if the conversational space feels conflictual, people won't step into it with you. If it feels safe, they will—and that is the role of *reframing*. In reframing, you give the person you are talking with an opportunity to mentally take a break and think in a new way. Reframing can change the context and give new meaning to a situation.

Take the following exchange as an example:

COMMENT: "I don't feel good about myself because I make so many mistakes." (The person may be in a fear state.)

REFRAMING: "Those who make mistakes are taking risks—and that is how we learn. People who take risks and make mistakes have a higher chance of finding the best new ways to do things. Edison made nine hundred light bulbs before finding the one that worked." (You are elevating the person into a trusting state using Level III sharing and reframing the context.)

Refocusing

Refocusing is another conversational tool that allows you to elevate people out of the place where they are stuck and point them toward another part of a larger topic where they can see connections they had not seen before. There are parts of the brain that are keenly designed by nature to help us focus, refocus, and even defocus. The reticular activating system (RAS) in the brain, which emanates out of the brain stem, is an energy system that enables us to guide our minds and focus our intention. When we do so, our brain defocuses on specific things and focuses instead on others. The RAS is thought of as an *intentional* system.

Consider the following as an example:

COMMENT: "I am really annoyed about how much time you spend on these small projects that don't seem to go anywhere. And you keep reworking them over and over and over." (The person may be stuck in a worry state and be fearful of not getting it right.)

REFOCUSING: "You really seem to care a lot about these projects. They must be really important to you. I'd love for you to apply your care about your work to a number of new projects rather than just a few small ones. This will allow you to expand your areas of focus and attention. My guess is you have a lot of great expertise now that you can bring to some new and challenging initiatives." (You are elevating the person's self-confidence, encouraging him to take more risks.)

Redirecting

Redirecting is another miraculous conversational tool for taking a difficult situation and turning it into an opportunity for finding trust and common ground with someone. Redirecting helps a person move from a place of being stuck and emotionally bound to a place where she can see new opportunities. This is such a great trust builder because it communicates that "I care enough about you to help you see things in a new light," rather than communicating a judgmental message that implies, "You Stupid Idiot."

Take, for example, the following comment:

COMMENT: "There is no way we can do anything other than what we did." (Stuck in the past.)

REDIRECTING: "Last week I worked with someone with the same issue and challenges you had. He, too, thought it was a dead end. Here is what he did. I never would have thought of it—but it really is amazing and offers a new way to look at things..." (Providing trusted insights to alternatives.)

The Road Map for Building Conversational Agility

When you notice that you are in a protective mode on the Conversational Dashboard, use reframing, refocusing, and redirecting to move yourself from the "Protect" side of the arc to the "Partner" side. When people are Resistors or Skeptics, they are either in a fear state or have apprehensions. They hang out to wait and see, and they watch what others do. Using your Conversational Intelligence skills, you can nudge them into Experimentor using reframing, refocusing, and redirecting. As you learn these skills, you will realize you are actually helping others create a mind shift from their lower brain—the reptilian brain—to their higher brain—the executive brain. Using the ARC of Engagement, you can refocus your conversations to elevate the communication abilities of everyone involved, even when dealing with difficult subjects. I call this a Leadershift.

Leadershift #1: From Fear to Transparency

When you are in a state of fear, you can only see right in front of your nose. The hardwiring of your nervous system is built to protect you from physical harm, but also from psychological harm.

Transparency—*Making threats transparent and focusing on quelling fears shifts your neurochemistry. When fear emerges, have co-creating conversations with someone you trust. Ask the person to listen for opportunities to reduce the fear. Ask for help reframing the perceived threat and seeing it from a new perspective.*

Refocus on transparency to overcome threats. The reptilian brain responds to threats more quickly than any other part of the brain. When we can talk about what we find threatening, we create the space for trust to be born. When the environment feels safe enough that people can share their concerns, the amygdala's threat response is down-regulated, allowing the brain's neurochemistry of trust to carry the day. When we speak openly and honestly about difficult issues, we can start to see each other as people with similar concerns and needs. We can deal with what lies behind our fears. Teams bond as they realize they can work through difficult issues and still have strong, positive relationships.

In the first step toward trust, we address the need to protect. When we make fears transparent we create a safe space; now, instead of withdrawing into fear and judgment, we can begin to move toward each other. We bring the resistor on board.

To evoke transparency and trust building:

- Quell the amygdala, the part of the brain that is activated when we feel fear and distrust. Create an open environment where people can talk about their fears, concerns, and threats openly.
- Encourage open conversations about how to make the environment a safe place for sharing, discovering, and connecting. Deal with issues right away.
- Starting with the hiring process, create clear and accurate job descriptions and expectations for success and communicate with transparency to your candidates.
- Create a performance review model that clearly identifies levels of excellence in performance; then, openly communicate benchmarks for success to your employees.
- Provide support in the form of training and mentoring to help each person reach excellence.
- Create learning opportunities and provide encouragement and compassion throughout the learning process rather than criticism and judgment.
- Provide a process for establishing accountability throughout the organization; create guidance for aligning words, actions, and deeds.
- Encourage conversations that promote transparency and trust.

Leadershift #2: From Power to Relationship Building

When you are feeling insecure about how you can contribute to a group, you may be fearful your voice will not be heard and thus be afraid of speaking up. Alternatively, you may fight to be heard and start to push too hard; you may move into a power stance, judging others critically or pushing them away. People may react to your power shift and respond in kind, creating a political environment and a cascade of unintended negative consequences.

Relationship building shifts your neurochemistry— *When power issues emerge, have a co-creating conversation with someone you trust. Connect with the person openly about the challenges you are facing. Ask for his neutral perspective: ask him to listen to you and reflect back your concerns—to be receptive and open, not judgmental. This will quell your amygdala and open the space to release some of your worries and concerns.*

Refocus on relating to others. Reaching out to connect is vital to establishing trust. Relationships hold people together. The entertainment company's leadership team realized that they had never addressed this fundamental issue. All too often, they had focused on their roles—their titles, status, and importance—rather than on forging genuine relationships. When I performed my discovery interviews at the media company, I found that people were fighting over who had the best parking spot! When people value relationships over status, they stimulate the brain chemistry that supports nurturing. They move from a fearful state of mind to a more trusting state of mind. Even in the face of difficult challenges, focusing on relationships shifts the conversation, which shifts the outcomes. As we will see, when relationships start to go bad in a healthy company, people use the tool of priming to address the issue quickly and directly. They focus on raising the bar on what good and great relationships look like—they focus on mutual support and understanding rather than personal gain.

When we focus on relationships first, we create a safe space for connecting with others heart to heart, and people move toward one another with compassion and understanding rather than away from each other in fear and judgment. We bring the skeptic on board.

To nurture and sustain relationships:

- Decide on the core values that will guide your organization's actions and its agreements with and between leaders, employees, vendors, and customers.
- Encourage conversations that demonstrate the value of the relationships.
- Ensure that each person feels that she "belongs" and has a role in the organization or team.
- Establish and practice rules of engagement that foster open, candid, and caring conversations.
- Learn to give feedback when relationships go off track, so that you can bring them back on track right away.

Leadershift #3: From Uncertainty to Understanding

When we are uncertain of the cultural norms and how we fit in, another defensive routine emerges: we give up and give in, and we accept the status quo. Uncertainty causes fear and anxiety, and it often sends us into a state of distrust. When that happens, find people to connect with to ensure you don't become isolated or feel left out, which will send you back into protective behaviors. Notice when you *impose* yourself on your relationships you may cause "tissue rejection"—by forcing yourself on others or on situations, you can cause others to instinctively reject your inclusion in the same way a skin graft can be rejected by the body.

Understanding needs and aspirations shifts your neuro-chemistry—*When you see that you are starting to make up stories to help you interpret another's actions and are creating movies with an "us against them" theme, or when you are feeling diminished in status or left out, have a co-creating conversation with someone you trust. Connect with her openly about the challenges you are facing, and have her ask you about your needs and* *aspirations for the future. What role do you want to play? What contribution do you want to make? What would you like to accomplish next? Then ask the person to listen to you and reflect back your needs, aspirations, hopes, and dreams, not to judge them. This will quell your amygdala and activate your prefrontal cortex, which is where new visions for the future reside.*

Refocus on understanding to minimize uncertainty. Our neocortex responds after the amygdala and heart, and brings in language to make sense of what is happening. Understanding is our friend, and uncertainty our enemy. When people are insecure about their role, where they fit in, and how they can rise to the next level, or if they are unsure of where the company is going and where they fit into the story, they fall prey to uncertainty. *Uncertainty is the fulcrum between distrust and trust.* Uncertainty is a clue that tells us we need to pay attention to building a deeper understanding of one another so we can move forward in the trust-building process. When we focus on down-regulating our fears and up-regulating our need to understand and be understood, we are literally rebalancing our neurochemistry. When we start to understand each other's needs and aspirations, we move from an I-centric mind-set to a WE-centric mind-set, and we start to believe that mutual success is possible.

When we focus on understanding the needs and aspirations of others, we create a safe space for people to feel they belong in the same team. We bring the person whose stance is "wait and see" on board.

To share views, perspectives, and aspirations as a way of increasing understanding:

- Listen to connect, not to reject.
- Make it a practice to ask for and listen to feedback from peers, employees, vendors, customers, competitors, and others who may not agree with your perspective and points of view.

- Consciously form work teams with people of different backgrounds, thought processes, experience levels, ages, and viewpoints.
- Allow people to fully express themselves through speaking, writing, and/or demonstrating their abilities.
- Make it a practice to ask "What if?" questions that open the doors to new ways of thinking without prejudging ideas that may be different from your own.

Leadershift #4: From a Need to Be Right to Mapping Shared Success

The desire to be right is a defensive routine that prevents you from seeing and hearing others' best thinking; when you are caught up in being right, you are defending your own point of view and living inside of your own story. You are often not even able to hear what your heart knows. Instead, you are only about being right—which makes others wrong. When you are advocating your own position extensively, you lose connectivity to others and break rapport. When rapport is broken our "distrust antenna" wakes up.

Sharing stories of mutual success shifts your neurochemistry—*Step back from your position and become curious about others' perspectives, knowledge, and successes. This intentional shift releases dopamine, which creates curiosity in your brain. When you are curious and ask questions of others, the heart connects to your brain, engaging you to open up. When this happens it sends a whole new bath of neurotransmitters that enable you to connect with others. Talk about mutual success. Define success together, make meaning together, and create the story together that describes the reality you want to co-create. This stimulates more oxytocin and will create new bonds of friendship, trust, and understanding.*

Refocus on shared success, which minimizes threats to self-interest. As we make sense of where we fit in and find our place in the evolving story, we need to join with others to create a sense of shared reality. Sharing with others is part of our fundamental need for community, but for many of us that need has been obscured by fear. Once we've cleared away our fears we can see that sharing is a basic benefit that allows us all to gain from being in this group together. We still take care of our own needs, but we do so with an eye on the needs of the entire group, secure in the feeling that we've got one another's backs. We move from judging others to appreciating the contributions made by all. When the team sees the value of working together, fears of fitting in are replaced by a state of connectivity and coherence that creates an extraordinary capacity for making rapid, unified decisions, even when complexity and chaos reign. As the team gels, the benefits of working together become clearer and clearer.

When we focus on working with others and define what success looks like together, we feel safer and stronger than we did when we were flying solo. In this safe environment we can also feel stronger in our convictions and in our own intuition. We've created space for the experimentor to come on board.

To create a sense of shared success that acknowledges the contributions made by all:

- Initiate conversations about mutual success and what success looks like for each of us.
- Encourage people at all levels to communicate and discuss the shared view of success with others.
- Encourage people at all levels to take ownership for their areas of contribution.
- Reward people for stepping outside their area of responsibilities to lend a hand or act as a sounding board for others in the pursuit of achieving mutual success.
- Celebrate the successes large and small.
- Acknowledge the value of everyone on the team.

Leadershift #5: From Groupthink to Group Cohesion and Partnering

When groupthink is a defensive routine and when it takes over a meeting or a conversation, people often give up sharing some of their best thinking in exchange for belonging to the tribe's way of thinking. Our hearts want to be in sync with others. You can contribute a tremendous amount by cultivating behaviors that ensure both belonging and having a voice, two of the most powerful needs of human beings.

Truth and consequences shift your neurochemistry—
Step back from the conversation and ask people to take time out to reflect on their decisions. Ask them to step aside from what they agreed upon to see if there is anything that was left behind—any great idea that was overlooked. Look for gaps, and work the gaps between reality and perception. This gives people permission to bring forward ideas that could benefit the whole group that might have been left behind. This narrows the gaps and reframes them from "my idea" to "our idea," and keeps the conversation open to go to a higher level of group processing.

Refocus on truth telling to close reality gaps. Our prefrontal cortex helps us make sense of reality; it controls how we create the stories we share with others and how we create the future. Our minds are like moviemakers, always striving to put what we learn into a coherent narrative: we're always trying to make sense of things. Unfortunately, as we know, our movies don't always sync up with the stories others tell. Two siblings with the same alcoholic parent can come away from their childhood experience with very different stories. One can go through every moment of every day waiting for the floor to drop out from under her, and the other can become a leader known for her resourcefulness. Even when our movies start off with the same basic elements, our stories can take very different directions. I call these differences reality gaps. They're inevitable, but when we share our movies with each other we become aware of those gaps. And when we take the next step—working together to create a movie that we truly share—we can work wonders.

Working together to create a movie that includes a vision for our company, a vision for today that extends into tomorrow, creates a space for trust that we can live in together. Now we are in the highest and most productive stage of trust building, in which co-creation becomes possible. Now we are free to function together at our most creative, in an environment that is devoted to evolution and growth.

When we focus on sharing our movies with each other to narrow the reality gaps, we create a safe space for people to feel they can partner with others and make great things happen. Now we've brought ourselves on board as co-creators of a healthy, prosperous future.

To get at "the truth" with candor and caring:

- Acknowledge that your truth may not be the only truth.
- Help others see that their truth may not be the only truth.
- Keep an open mind of discovery in the pursuit of truth.
- Discuss gaps between "your truth" and "my truth," with the intention of creating bridges of understanding (closing reality gaps).
- Encourage conversations that start with empathy and move toward a common goal or outcome.
- Speak and show appreciation to others for their efforts and successes.

Learning How to Rebound

As we begin to understand that trust is the foundation of our connection with others and work to master the skills of Conversational Intelligence, we learn to build trusting relationships with others more quickly and to tap our collective intelligence at the same time. We experience a new power over our minds and our conversations; we become navigators of a larger universe of possibilities for bringing new levels of trust and value to our teams, our companies, our brands, and ourselves. We can also learn to rebound and to rebuild trust even when it has been lost or has not been co-created.

In the next chapter, we'll explore exercises and tools to help us achieve higher levels of Conversational Intelligence across an organization. Then we'll move into the final section of this book, which features success stories of companies that moved from "Protect" to "Partner" by using Level III interaction dynamics to activate higher levels of Conversational Intelligence.

9

A Toolkit for Level III Conversations

What counts in making a happy relationship is not so much how compatible you are, but how you deal with incompatibility.

—DANIEL GOLEMAN

The exercises in this Conversational Intelligence Toolkit are mental and conversational rituals that will help you deconstruct conversations and learn to reframe, refocus, and redirect them. By using higher levels of conversational dynamics, you can move into higher levels of engagement as you learn to shape your interactions with others.

Engage in the Face of Conflict

Most of us experience moments of conflict every week, if not every day. One of my clients and I coined an expression to describe this—you fall prey to the three Ps: power, politics, and personalities. These are the moments when you disagree with someone on an important issue, get triggered, and then go for a win. If the conflict involves something very important to you, you can feel yourself sliding back into a Level II conversation, taking a position and fighting for your beliefs. I have a great exercise for you to do when you find yourself in this position;

this exercise will help you stay in your neutral Third Eye, and use a "sharing and discovering" approach to build understanding about the other person's perspectives so he feels heard, not threatened. As you strengthen your relationships with others by listening and caring, you quell your amygdala and theirs, trigger your mirror neuron system and theirs, create greater levels of empathy, and open your executive brain to thinking about conflicts in new ways. As you trigger higher levels of oxytocin—the trust and bonding hormone—a conflict can turn into an opportunity to open new possibilities for both you and the person you disagree with. This amazing exercise is called Double-Clicking. Once you learn how to Double-Click—and the process is laid out below using an example—you will find you can integrate this process into your conversations with people at times of conflict. Or you can use it when you need to get inside another point of view to gain greater empathy for another person's perspectives, needs, and aspirations.

Double-Clicking Exercise

Double-Clicking came to me after I observed and studied the difference between two executives in conversation and between teams that were successful and those that were not. I call it "Double-Clicking" because the process mimics opening folders on your computer to drill down into details. Double-Clicking enables each person to unlock the deeper connections she is making that others may not. When I use this approach with teams, I ask them to delve into their individual mindscapes to share and compare word meanings and perceptions with each other.

To do this exercise, group people into teams of five to seven people. Working in teams allows people to share and compare their versions of Double-Clicking with each other. It makes the exercise more engaging and breaks down barriers. Ask each person to draw a circle in the center of a piece of paper. In the middle of the circle, write the word "Success," then draw twelve spokes around the circle so it looks like a clock. At each of the twelve spokes ask people to write one word that represents success to them.

Ask people in the group to share the twelve words that embody success for them. If your group is like the thousands of others with whom I've done this exercise, you will discover that when people share and compare their spokes, few have words that describe success that are similar to others' descriptions. One person may view team success as a lack of conflict, another may see it as the ability to share different ideas and challenge each other, and another might view it using only a financial measure.

What does this mean? It means that we assume we are aligned around success when we are not. Our success wheels represent the way we measure success, how we envision success, and how we navigate to create success. If our movies differ in the specifics, it's no wonder we create cultures of distrust. I'm looking to produce my movie of success while you are looking to produce yours.

When we Double-Click on core ideas to discover their meanings, we will not find just a list of bullet points or a set of steps to follow. As we Double-Click on ideas with others, we are unfolding our unique mindscapes and sharing our view of the world—perhaps publicly for the first time. Inside any Double-Click is a unique combination of links and associations that make up each person's singular view of the world. When we Double-Click on a word or concept, we display our mindscapes for all to see. These associations reflect our view of the world, and this view is often something we haven't examined until the Double-Click exercise.

From Conflict to Co-creation

Double-Clicking is an antidote to conflict. When you look inside someone else's meanings of words, you will see that conflicts often come from the way we frame or define the words we use. What people learn through this exercise is how to practice living in *discovery*, both for themselves and with others. When we don't stop to explore and discover, we live with the belief that we disagree, when in fact we may not.

I knew there was something neurochemical going on in the minds and hearts of my clients when we graphically mapped "success" together. We could feel an organic and chemical change taking place that turned foes into friends and transformed "my ideas" into "our ideas." It was a dramatic shift that moved us from I to WE—a shift that is at the heart of Conversational Intelligence. Creating WE is a neurochemical shift that takes place inside people and enables higher levels of bonding and collaboration.

The premise of this exercise is that we all hold different views of reality, and when we Double-Click, we explore the unique connections at the heart of the matter. We are able to breathe new life and possibilities into a business and into relationships—the first step to creating organizational transformation. Our research has shown that successful teams take the time to align their thinking in many ways. When they do, they begin to operate in a more coherent way—their hearts and minds get into sync.

Level III conversations promote a rich dialogue in which you ask questions for which you have no answers, share and discover what is on your mind, and encourage everyone to help shape mutual success. These sorts of dialogues change an environment driven by the three Ps —power, politics, and personalities—into an environment that *honors the Is inside the WEs.* By giving everyone a chance to talk about mutual success and build a shared "movie" of what success looks like, the interaction dynamics change and the neurochemical drivers behind interactions change too. Most of all, Level III conversations reduce the levels of uncertainty that trigger distrust and create a process that allows everyone to play a role in defining success for the whole enterprise. Level III goes well beyond Level II. It activates the transformational capabilities hardwired into our brains, catalyzing new neuronal connections and creating a brain alchemy that enables us to evolve our thinking alongside others'. This level of conversation is so powerful that it activates an energy that, I believe, shapes new DNA. Below are more conversational rituals that elevate us into Level III.

Double-Click to Reshape the Future

More than a decade ago, when I was first testing the idea of Double-Clicking, I tried it with one of my senior executive women's initiatives. This group was quite special. It consisted of women leaders who were colleagues in the field of communications. The group met monthly to inspire and support one another's growth in their organizations. None of them worked for the same company, however all were in the communications field. At this particular meeting, I asked the group to try my new exercise.

I asked each person to draw a circle in the center of a piece of paper and to write the words "Financial Success" in the middle of the circle. Their task was to come up with as many associations with Financial Success as they could. They could use arrows to connect ideas and draw lines or double lines to show strength of connections—they could diagram in any way they needed to in order to bring the connections between ideas to life.

I am certain what happened at that meeting was as surprising for them as it was for me. What we discovered when looking at the results was that there were deep connections among ideas inside their minds that they didn't know existed.

Through the Double-Clicking exercise, some of the women discovered that, deep in the unexplored recesses of their minds, were fears about making money. These were fears that were holding them back, fears that were sending them unconscious signals telling them they could not build their financial platform. What a big aha moment, not just for one or two women but for the whole room.

Double-Clicking has become central to my work, regardless of the size of the company or the complexity of the project. Double-Clicking is a powerful tool for looking inside the core concepts that hold a relationship, team, and organization together. We all hold different views of reality, and when we look inside to see the meanings we make of core concepts, we discover associations we didn't know we had. When I use Double-Clicking as part of my client projects, it brings to light areas where people are aligned and areas where they are not, knowledge that is the first step in creating organizational transformation. In the next section of this chapter you'll find more powerful conversational tools for harvesting business success.

Evolving Insights and Wisdom

Often, we find ourselves in Level I transactional conversations in our day-to-day work. We update each other, pass along information necessary to do our jobs, and then move on to the next task. Our meetings can become transactional also, checking things off to-do lists and not linking back with others until the next meeting. Later, we may discover that the takeaways we thought were shared by everyone in the meeting were actually not aligned.

By bringing Level III conversational dynamics into our meetings, even in small ways, or through conversational rituals such as the LEARN exercise that follows, we can enhance each other's connectivity, insight, wisdom, and shared view of success. We can also share our fears and concerns, sustaining a more transparent workplace so that we don't harbor fears and anxieties but rather harvest insights and wisdom.

LEARN Exercise

With every meeting, major decision, or conversation, or even big organizational initiatives, you can enhance the levels of trust and decrease the levels of fear and distrust by doing an end-of-meeting activity. This activity gives everyone in the meeting a chance to exercise Level III dynamics and recalibrate their understanding of the meeting's content—it lets people share what they liked and didn't and create next steps that are meaningful for everyone.

This exercise also signals the amygdala to slow down and be quiet, and it allows people in the room to engage in the process of "coherence" or of getting in sync with others at the heart level. Heart brain connection is very powerful and sends signals to the rest of the brain that all is well and we are okay with one another. Using the acronym LEARN, go around the room and ask people to speak to the letters of the word:

L = Like: what did you like most about this meeting?

E = Excite: what excited you most?

A = Anxiety: what created the greatest anxiety?

R = Reward: what can we celebrate about the way we handled this meeting? (Or you can use other "Rs" based on the type of meeting: what do you now want to reframe, revision, redirect, restore, etc.)

N = Need: what are the next steps we need to take to stay on track?

Transforming Anger into Alignment

Sometimes we unintentionally anger someone or we say the wrong thing or we get into a conflict without meaning to. This may happen at work, with customers, with friends, or within our own family. Conversational rituals can become part of everyday life to support people in bridging, connecting, and strengthening their relationships.

Make Up Exercise

When you make a mistake with a partner, a customer, or someone you care about and you fix it, you make that person happy. "Service recovery" is the term for accepting a problem and agreeing to fix it or for apologizing for an inconvenience and righting it. We appreciate it when others take responsibility for their actions and do something about it. When, on the other hand, we defend ourselves and try to explain why we did whatever upset the other person, we blow it. People don't care why something happened; they just want the problem resolved.

The same is true in all our relationships. If we step on someone's toes, we can usually make up by saying we are sorry—by apologizing—and promising not to do it again. My husband taught our children a game when they were little. It was called the "Make Up Game." When they got into fights and couldn't stop, he taught them the steps to work it out, and made a game of it to take the sting out of having to apologize. The Make Up Game works with everyone. It may sound childish at first, but I've taught this game to executives around the world, and they have told me how much it has helped them turn a "cold" relationship into a "warm" one. Here is how it works:

- Ask: Are we in a fight (or having issues)? Let's talk. What do you need to get off your chest?
- Then listen. Appreciate the other person's point of view. (Don't judge.)
- Ask: What can I do for you (change, stop doing, start doing) to make it better? What do you need from me? This is what I need from you. (This is where you help each other turn emotions into positive

requests for what to do differently in the future. You learn to verbalize what you need and want—this is really healthy.)

- Ask: How much longer are you going to be mad? One hour? Two? This is a "pattern interrupt," and the touch of humor resets our brain and enables us to refocus on more constructive outcomes. It quells the amygdala and enables the prefrontal cortex to regain its focus on the situations quickly and in a constructive way.
- Agree: When you are finished discussing the conflict, one person says, "You say Make." The other says, "You say Up."

This is what kids do. Adults may want to shake hands and say something like, "Thanks for the talk" or say, "This was really helpful to me. How was it for you?" If both parties can't shake hands and express such feelings, you are not finished talking. You'll know when you've reached the destination.

Harvesting Insights, Wisdom, and New Perspectives

I remember a conversation with a professor who said, "Life can hit us like an asteroid." We are just at the wrong place at the wrong time or we are in an emotional state that takes us out, and we are not the sensitive, caring person we want to be. We all have scars and experiences that leave an imprint on us that we keep recycling in our brain over and over again.

Life is an uncertain evolution and requires we spend much of our time in a state of experimentation. In Dan Coyle's book *The Talent Code*, he researched hotbeds of intelligence to find the patterns that enabled people to become great in their field. He studied academics, athletes, businesspeople in companies around the world, and people with extraordinary music talent. Coyle learned that people who achieve a level of greatness in their field shared a skill I call "Look Back to Look Forward." When these people made mistakes, they developed an instant response: they stepped outside their own experience in that moment, and saw the event not as a mistake, which is judgment, but rather as a neutral way to learn from what went wrong. They then reset their minds to incorporate this new learning and began to use it immediately—trying it out, anchoring it in their repertoire, and moving on.

When we live in Level III conversational dynamics we learn to change how we think and communicate, not only with others but also with ourselves. You can do the next exercise alone or with others. It helps you Look Back to Look Forward—to rewrite your story about key events in your life so you come away with insights, wisdom, and new meaning.

Looking Back to Look Forward Exercise

This is a powerful exercise that can help you take away new meanings and interpretations from past experiences, even those about which you harbor negativity and bad feelings. This exercise also rebuilds a sense of personal and organizational trust. It is based on the fact that too often we hold on to the past. It's all we know. What we hold in our minds is our reality. Sometimes our reality is full of anger, retribution, and disappointment. When we project this onto others we feel distrust for the future. Yet at moments of contact we can choose to share and compare what we think, believe, and honor with others. When we do this we take a big step forward, reframing what we thought was reality and realizing that each of us has our own view of reality to share with others.

In this exercise you choose events in your life that are significant. Write them down, and then ask the event, "What are you here to teach me?" Ask for wisdom to take forward with you on your journey. Rather than bringing along the negative feelings, use reframing to revisit the way you think about the situation and to extract lessons to take forward. This process releases "Amygdala Hijack" and moves you into accessing your prefrontal cortex, where you can gain new wisdom for the road. When we take the time to look back to look forward we are able to glean new insights from our own history and from that of others whose perspective we value.

Back to the Future Exercise

In 1987 I created my Back to the Future exercise (a variation on my Looking Back to Look Forward Exercise) for one hundred and eighty very powerful CEOs. I was really worried when I introduced this exercise. It was the first time I'd stood up in front of senior executives I didn't know to lead an exercise I created that I had never tested before. As it turned out, the exercise stirred many hearts and minds in a good way. I thought I might be labeled "soft" by doing this exercise, but something told me to do it anyway (that is my rebel standing up for my beliefs).

By the end of the hour-long exercise, I discovered that the executives were in a new state of mind. After the event, people came over to me and thanked me for opening them up to themselves.

Step 1: *Create a Lifeline*

On a piece of paper, positioned horizontally, lay out your lifeline by segmenting the sheet into segments starting from the left: the first third of your life, second third, and last third. You can also do this in quarters.

Step 2: *Identify Situations, People, or Events That Had a Big Impact*

Reflect on your life in terms of these time segments and identify key events that had a big impact on you. Mark them on the paper with some key words to anchor them. Visit each time segment and find at least one event in that time frame.

The key event will have:

- Key situation
- Key people and/or "board of advisors"
- Story you made up about the event
- Key takeaways and lessons

After identifying your timeline stories, share them with a partner.

Step 3: *Patterns and Meaning Making*

Share your whole lifeline from the past to the present with your partner. You will share your situation, people, story, and key lessons learned, one at a time, until you have covered your whole timeline. After each sharing, ask your partner if he saw any patterns or interesting effects that you may not have seen. Share all your events with your partner and step back with him as you get to the present and see the larger patterns in your life. Capture insights.

Step 4: *Back to the Future*

Each partner then takes a turn looking into the future to see what's next. How is this life pattern going to impact your future? Is there a pattern that you want to replicate, change, or do differently? Draw out wisdom for your life's journey.

Step 5: *Map Making*

Reflect on your life from the larger perspective. Are there any other things that this exercise can teach you that can enhance your personal or professional life? What are your biggest takeaways?

Step 6: *Trust in the Future*

This last step is a chance for you and your coaching partner to reflect on and take away learnings for the future. How can you show appreciation for your coaching partner's story? How can you acknowledge his commitment to his own future? How can you acknowledge her trust in herself?

Level Setting an Organization

Power, politics, and personalities are part of being human. We are, by nature, pack animals, and we have evolved to function better when we are inside a group rather than outside. There is no way we can turn off a switch and stop wanting to be included, appreciated, valued, and to have status in our organizations.

By becoming a master of Conversational Intelligence—recognizing the level at which conversations are taking place and enhancing the quality of the engagement at each level—you will become a driving force of meaningful conversations in your organization and in your life.

Becoming astute and insightful about the appropriate levels of Conversation Intelligence at the appropriate times will help us level set our conversations for the right purpose. Developing your Third Eye is a skill that will enable you to master all three levels. As you learn to step back and see the dynamics needed and successfully marry your intention and impact to shape the conversational space for desired outcomes, you will find your proficiency at moving into Level III interactions will soar.

PART III

Getting to the Next Level of Greatness

10

Leading with Trust: Laying the Foundation for Level III Interactions

Times of stress and difficulty are seasons of opportunity when the seeds of progress are sown.

—THOMAS F. WOODLOCK

Among my clients are some of the most courageous, wisdom-driven executives I've ever met. I always come away smarter and more open to learning when I work with them. Just by observing them in action, I have learned how to plant, fertilize, and harvest Conversational Intelligence in organizations. This chapter outlines how leaders learn to activate Level III trust networks, shifting a whole organization from distrust to trust and transforming a culture.

Trust Is the Foundation of Great Leadership

Change is the nature of every successful company's journey. When the market shifts, successful companies need to be agile; they must be able to get in front of the curve and succeed time and again.

Change brings with it uncertainty, and uncertainty triggers fear. As leaders learn to reduce fear and increase trust within their organizations, they lay

CONVERSATIONAL INTELLIGENCE

the foundation for higher-level conversations, where opportunities for greater innovation, collaboration, and success are revealed. As Boris Groysberg and Michael Slind expressed in their book, *Talk, Inc.*, leaders who engage their organizations in conversations that reflect intimacy, inclusion, interactivity, and intentionality are able to bring people together and integrate their efforts.

As leaders learn to shift their interaction dynamics from Level I to III, an amazing thing happens. There is an alchemical change in their culture, one that can happen instantly. As leaders step into Level III, they bring people with them. They create a conversational space that allows people to share what's on their minds with candor and caring, they create conversational agility that nurtures people's ability to handle the unexpected, and they harvest wisdom and insights.

Angelika Dimoka, PhD and Paul Pavlou, PhD, both professors at the Fox School of Business at Temple University, are directing some of their work toward integrating research in the areas of trust and neural decision-making. This work is housed in the Department of Neural Decision-making at Temple. I had the opportunity to interview them for a TV segment for a global program I've co-created with the National Constitution Center in Philadelphia. At the end of the interview, I summarized our conversation by pulling out the following vital insight that is at the heart of this book: we are hardwired with the capacity for both trust and distrust to help us deal with uncertainty. When uncertainty shows up we can move into either protective behaviors to ensure survival, or we can move into trust behaviors to bond with others. Both trust and distrust give us strategies for uncertainty, and uncertainty is a way of life—it will never go away. Those leaders who are most successful use trust-building behaviors even in the face of uncertainty.

How Great Leaders Get Extraordinary Results

Consider the challenges Angela Ahrendts faced when she became CEO of Burberry in 2006. This 150-plus-year-old, tradition-rich British company was languishing in a sector that was flourishing, even after a turn around by her predecessor.

In 2011, just five years after Angela came onboard, Burberry was lauded as the fourth-fastest-growing brand after Apple, Google, and Amazon by both WPP/BrandZ and Interbrand, who also ranked it as the world's fastest-growing fashion brand the following year. By 2013, Fast Company named Burberry the second most innovative retail company globally. How did Ahrendts accomplish this extraordinary feat? The answer lies in raising her organization's Conversational Intelligence.

Many leaders say that having one conversation across an organization is not possible. Yet Ahrendts challenged that belief, and put her own Conversational Intelligence to the test. A truly collaborative leader, Ahrendts didn't do this alone. The thought of engaging nine thousand people globally in one conversation might seem daunting to many, if not most, leaders. Yet Ahrendts knew that breaking down walls of distrust and harnessing the collective wisdom and intelligence of her organization was her primary task if she was going to be a success—if Burberry was going to be a success.

Ahrendts realized when she joined Burberry that there was a huge amount of work to be done. The company was languishing, the culture was broken, and Burberry's future was unclear. Ahrendts became CEO after a six-month transition period during which she shadowed her predecessor Rose Marie Bravo, which allowed her to understand the challenges of the culture, and the people she would be working with. With this knowledge, she began to formulate the strategies that would eventually transform a sleeping giant into a fast-growing, digital, luxury company.

The gap between what Ahrendts discovered at Burberry and what she wanted to do was huge. The company ended the year up 2 percent and the luxury goods sector as a whole was up about thirteen percent. The company had gone public a month before Ahrendts joined. She and her management team got together and said, "How can we create the greatest team and the greatest company?"

"We started to ask, who are we?" Ahrendts remembers. "And who are we becoming?" She knew it was her mission both to protect a legacy company and to help it launch an exciting and growth-oriented future. She and her team asked, "How can we sustain our company for another 150 years?" The solution they evolved was to marry classic style and tradition with the young and digital—and focus on elevating their organizational teamwork.

Cultural, Emotional, and Organizational Redesign

Just as a designer creates a new product line or a tech guru engages an organization in inventing the next-generation device, Ahrendts focused first on assembling her team. Her most important move was to promote Christopher Bailey to chief creative officer. Ahrendts often referred to Bailey as the "brand czar," so that he had the freedom to invent a new company rather than feel bound by the past. One of the powerful things we are learning in the world of Conversational Intelligence is that when a person's title changes, it opens up a new part of his brain.

The labels we put on others and ourselves influence the way we act, think, and behave. They influence what we give ourselves permission to think and how we limit our thinking. Neuroscientists have discovered, by using fMRI scans, that every person we interact with holds a place in our brain. With every interaction, we add more data points to that place in our brain, and we collect perceptions, feelings, and memories. When we see that person again, we call up those memory clusters and we know the person. If we have a lot of good feelings associated with her, we are flushed with feel-good hormones, but if the person makes us feel bad, we are flushed with feel-bad hormones.

When Ahrendts gave Bailey a new title that had no history within the company, it freed him to invent and develop his role with much grander potential—and he grew into his new shoes with gusto.

Bailey had the vision, and the more Ahrendts trusted him and challenged him by giving him more responsibility, the more he rose to the occasion. Then Ahrendts promoted her chief technology officer to work with Bailey. "I wanted John to drive the business with Christopher," she recounted, "marrying creative and technology." This brought two talented people together to co-create Burberry's new future.

Ahrendts knew she had to nurture unconventional relationships so people could learn to work together in unconventional ways. Merging technology and creative aspects and promoting their runway shows globally on the Web not only created a conversation internally, it created a conversation externally with the customer. Early on, Ahrendts created a strategic innovative council. Bailey chaired that group and selected "digital natives"—younger employees within the company who had grown up with digital technology—to offer ideas about how the company could evolve. They presented these ideas to the Strategic Innovative Council, and their job was to execute their young vision, passing it through the filter of their experience. "We flipped the traditional hierarchy," Ahrendts remembers, "and we involved ideas from the next generation so they could have a voice. It was a revolutionary idea."

Trust Is the Heart of It All

Visiting with Ahrendts and her senior team on a number of occasions, I was able to see Level III interaction dynamics in action. Ahrendts had her mind set on engaging the whole organization in one conversation about the business and where it was going. She knew from growing up in other companies that when the *one conversation* breaks down and there are many conversations, a culture becomes fragmented and fragile. When people are confused about whose voice to listen to, a culture becomes an exaggerated worst-case scenario of Level II positional dynamics. Employees engage in a lot of behind-the-scenes positioning, silos emerge, and work slows down.

Ahrendts, deeply steeped in Level III transformation dynamics, knew that everything starts with a foundation of trust, and so she set her sights high and began *priming* the organization for connectivity, trust, and innovation. She put it this way:

> "Trust is truly at the heart of it all. If trust is your core value, you hire accordingly. I interviewed a lot of senior management people, and at this level competence and experience are a given; trust is the difference-maker. When I look them in the eye I'm asking myself: Do I trust them, and do I get the feeling that they trust me? Do they get the vision? This is the starting point for everything we do."

Trust is the glue that holds an organization together in the face of enormous challenges. Trust *primes the pump* so that people can get intimate and feel open enough to be inclusive, interactive, and intentional.

Trust looks like this: I trust that you and I share the same view of reality. I trust that you will have my best interests at heart (you care about me); that you will not cause me to fear you; you will allow me to speak without fear of retribution so I can be open and candid with you and share everything that's on my mind. (You demonstrate that you are my friend, not my foe.)

Distrust looks like this: You and I see the world very differently. We disagree on what's important. I feel you have your own interests at heart and could care less about mine. You talk out of two sides of your mouth—one to me, and another to your closest buddies. I am afraid to share what's on my mind for fear you'll use it against me. (In truth, you act like a foe, not a friend.)

Human beings have a need to belong that is considered by neuroscientists and psychologists to be more powerful than the need for physical safety and security. Many organizations operate in a perpetual state of distrust and fear. A fearful state of mind alters the way we see and experience reality, the way we interact with others, and how much we are willing to engage, innovate, and speak our minds. *When trust is absent, we see REALITY with threatened eyes, and we:*

- R*eveal less* than what we know or what is helpful to move forward
- E*xpect more* than what is possible
- A*ssume the worst* of others
- L*ook at situations* with caution
- I*nterpret communications* with fear
- T*ell secrets* we promised not to tell
- Y*es people* to avoid confronting truth

When we are in a state of distrust, the world feels threatening. Threats make us retreat. They make us feel we need to protect ourselves. We are more sensitive to feeling wrong or embarrassed, and we behave differently. High levels of threat send us into Amygdala Hijack.

TRUST CHANGES REALITY

AMYGDALA HIJACK Cortisol		PREFRONTAL CORTEX Oxytocin
DISTRUST: we see reality through threats and fear and close down	Long-Range, Inclusive View / Far Sighted / Short Sighted / Near Sighted	**TRUST:** we see reality more clearly and are more open to engage
Reveal less **E**xpect more **A**ssume the worst **L**ook with caution **I**nterpret with fear **T**ell secrets **Y**es people	*Different Mind-Sets*	**R**eveal more **E**xpect less & over deliver **A**ssume the best **L**ook with an open heart **I**nterpret with facts **T**ell the truth **Y**es to confronting the truth

FIGURE 10–1: Views of REALITY

Yet when we are in a state of trust, we experience reality with new eyes and we:

- Reveal more
- Expect less and over deliver
- Assume the best of others
- Look at situations with an open heart
- Interpret communications through truth and facts
- Tell the truth
- Yes people to confront truth

The kind of sweeping changes proposed by Ahrendts when she became CEO of Burberry could have felt incredibly threatening to the company's employees, as many organizations undergoing transformational change allow executives to retreat behind closed doors and distance front-line employees from decision making, effectively shutting down employees' ability to connect with leadership and limiting their ability to engage in co-creating conversations.

The difference at Burberry is that Ahrendts made a strategic decision to create a conversational forum that included everyone in the company. In the same way she used technology to connect with customers, she created a platform that encouraged people inside the company to communicate directly with her and with others on the senior team, moving employees essentially from the "protect" mode into a "share and co-create" mode. By creating a culture where everyone is empowered to share what's on their minds, she avoided the pitfalls of leaders who lose the benefit of valuable employees' ideas by not encouraging young, forward-looking managers to propose radical new ways of thinking about the business.

Ahrendts's focus on creating trust with her senior team and across her organization led Burberry through a total transformation, from an organization looking backward to one of the most dynamic retail and digital global brands today. Ahrendts wanted everyone within the company to be "cultivating the next-generation thinking." She related:

You should *feel* a culture, and a brand. A culture is a living brand. We said, "We will build the brand by building the culture. What's right for the brand?" It became a higher purpose. How could our employees help us create not only a **great** brand but also a great company?

We talk a lot about the Burberry brand. It's not about what's best for you; it's about what's best for the brand. And when there's no ego involved you can make the best possible decisions and move quickly to implement them. Humans are insecure by nature, so if you don't trust someone you can get lost in a perpetual loop of insecurity. But when you trust people to partner with you, you can share your insecurities and use them to build bridges. This openness and transparency connects us to each other in a totally new way. When you openly acknowledge you can't do it without the other person, ego gets replaced by the knowledge that we're all in this together.

The Seven Conversations

Conversational Intelligence is the power to elevate our collective intelligence. This is not IQ—it's C-IQ.

However, not all conversations are able to elevate C-IQ. For example, conversations that trigger exclusion and judgment cause us to recoil from speaking up and being fully engaged with others. Conversations that make us feel like our territory has been limited or taken away, and those in which we feel that people are withholding important information from us, cause us to feel we are not part of the team. Some conversations make us feel stupid or punish us for speaking up, and these send us into "flight, fight, freeze, or appease" behaviors, which are fueled by the primitive brain. Conversations that stir up self-doubt or cause us to want to get back at others trigger high emotions that block our best thinking.

The power of Level III interaction dynamics comes from their ability to catalyze the higher intelligence located in the prefrontal lobes, a type of intelligence we can only access if we feel good about others and ourselves. That is why Level III requires that the heart brain and the executive brain work in harmony.

To help you elevate your culture to Level III interaction dynamics, start engaging in the seven vital conversations outlined below. Each one facilitates your ability to access Conversational Intelligence and to enhance your powerful ability to co-create with others.

- Co-creating Conversations—catalyze functions in the prefrontal cortex that stimulate mirror neurons, which enable you to see the world through others' eyes
- Humanizing Conversations—catalyze functions in the prefrontal cortex that stimulate higher levels of empathy and candor
- Aspiring Conversations—catalyze functions in the prefrontal cortex that stimulate higher levels of foresight
- Navigating Conversations—catalyze functions in the prefrontal cortex that stimulate higher levels of collaboration
- Generating Conversations—catalyze functions in the prefrontal cortex that stimulate learning from mistakes
- Expressing Conversations—catalyze functions in the prefrontal cortex that stimulate higher levels of judgment and voice
- Synchronizing Conversations—catalyze functions in the prefrontal cortex that enable you to close the gaps between reality and aspirations

Ask yourself: What changes are you willing to make to elevate your culture to Level III?[1]

Co-creating Conversations

Are conversations in our organization healthy and inclusive? To what extent and in what ways are we fostering a vision for, and a climate of, inclusion rather than exclusion? To what extent are we inviting members of the organization to participate in defining the organization's vision and shared values? In co-creating the future, to what extent are we fostering a sense of community, connection, and engagement throughout the organization?

- *Be an inclusive Level III leader:* Foster conversations—share and discover so people can understand how they can participate in creating a great culture and community.
- *Action:* Shifting from *exclusion* to *inclusion* catalyzes Level III.

Humanizing Conversations

Are conversations appreciative? To what extent and in what ways are we setting the tone for colleagues to respect, honor, and appreciate rather than judge one another? In what ways are we fostering an environment that nurtures supportive, cooperative relationships through candor, caring, and openness?

- *Be an appreciative Level III leader:* Set the tone for open and honest communication, helping people learn how to express what they are feeling and to move from being politically driven to being trusting, candid, and caring.
- *Action:* Shifting from *judging* to *appreciating* catalyzes Level III.

Aspiring Conversations

Are conversations in our organization aspirational? To what extent and in what ways are we helping colleagues embrace the future rather than fear it? How are we helping people connect team and organizational expectations and goals with their own dreams, passions, and aspirations? How are we expanding people's sense of what is possible for themselves and the organization?

- *Be an aspirational Level III leader:* Are you limiting people's aspirations and leading them to lower their sights? Instead, help them to expand and embrace exciting and challenging possibilities.
- *Action:* Shifting from *limiting* to *expanding* catalyzes Level III.

Navigating Conversations

Do conversations foster collaboration and sharing across boundaries? To what extent and in what ways are we setting the tone for cross-organizational partnering? When, where, and how are colleagues invited to share information, exchange best practices, and reduce the need to protect turf? How are we helping the organization move from withholding to breaking down silos and exploring uncharted territories—both inside and outside the organization?

- *Be a trusted and collaborative Level III leader:* Share information, exchange best practices, reduce the need to protect turf, and break down silos to pioneer new territories.
- *Action:* Shifting from *withholding* to *sharing* catalyzes Level III.

Generating Conversations

Do conversations foster next-generation thinking? To what extent and in what ways are we helping colleagues move from being attached to the past and old grooves (knowing it all) to focusing on breakthrough ideas, innovations, and strategies? How are we fostering imagination, creativity, innovation, and generative thinking for growth both within the company and outside it with partners and customers?

- *Be a generative Level III leader:* Focus on innovative, creative, experimental, and generative ways of leading rather than relying on well-worn grooves.
- *Action:* Shifting from *having all the answers* to *discovering the new* catalyzes Level III.

Expressing Conversations

Do conversations communicate that everyone's voice counts? To what extent and in what ways are we working to develop the next generation of leaders? How are we fostering an environment in which people cultivate and communicate their own judgment and perspectives in their own unique voices? In what ways are we empowering people to challenge authority and avoid forced consensus or groupthink (a pattern of conformity to group norms)? How are we catalyzing people's leadership instincts and wisdom so everyone can contribute to the growth of the organization?

- *Be an influential Level III leader:* Teach people how to speak up, express their voice, challenge authority, and develop their ideas to contribute to the growth of the brand.
- *Action:* Shifting from *dictating* to *developing* catalyzes Level III.

Synchronizing Conversations

Do conversations in our organization celebrate success? To what extent and in what ways are we setting the tone for enterprise spirit, celebration, and reinvention, helping people move from the singular focus on "making the numbers" to seeking a higher mission and purpose? In what ways are people being nourished intellectually and spiritually—and nourishing others—while contributing to the ongoing evolution of the enterprise? How are we helping the enterprise achieve the next level of greatness?

- *Be an enterprise Level III leader:* Set the tone for an enterprise spirit, helping people move from a focus on "winning at all costs" or an "I win, you lose" attitude to a focus on contributing to their own growth in the context of enterprise growth.
- *Action:* Shifting from *compliance* to *celebration* catalyzes Level III.

Self-aware Level III leaders look inside and explore the dynamics of their own nature and the impact they have on their culture. They learn what it takes to create a culture that allows colleagues to be fully engaged and motivated.

Are you willing to examine your leadership and the way you influence your colleagues? When you influence in positive ways, you have a more profound impact on growth and you create a culture that sustains commitment and enthusiasm to achieve your vital strategies and goals.

Let's take a look at how Conversational Intelligence can help teams create extraordinary breakthroughs and results.

11

Teaming Up Through
Conversational Intelligence

We must learn to live together as brothers or perish together as fools.
—MARTIN LUTHER KING, JR.

In 1965, psychologist Bruce Tuckman, then a professor at Rutgers University and now head of the Academic Learning Lab at Ohio State University, introduced a theory about the developmental sequence of small groups. At the time, he proposed a very innovative model that has become the basis for almost all team and relationship development today. His model refers to four stages of team development: forming, storming, norming, and performing. Team members progress through these four stages as they learn to become high-performing, collaborative colleagues.

The Forming Stage

Tuckman asserts that in the *forming* stage, teams come together to work on projects. In the background, and in ways not always apparent, relationships are forming. People are watching to see who is in and who is

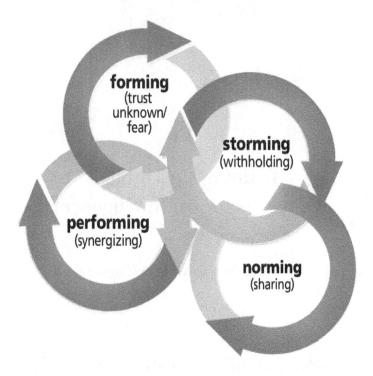

FIGURE 11–1: Forming, Storming, Norming, Performing

out—who is important and who is less important. Behavior is driven by a desire to be accepted by the others and to avoid controversy or conflict.

Trust is unknown and people have a combination of fear and expectation simultaneously. Because levels of uncertainty are high, both trust and distrust are being activated in the brain at the same time. Consequently, serious issues and feelings are avoided, and people focus on being busy with routines, such as team organization, who does what, and when to meet, which increases feelings of security and comfort.

While individuals are gathering information and impressions about one another, they are not addressing worries. Fears about loss or gain, concerns about how to fit in, and issues about power, who knows what, who is the smartest, and how to be a valued voice are pushed under the table rather than addressed in a candid and caring way. These are defen-

UNCERTAINTY AT THE MOMENT OF CONTACT

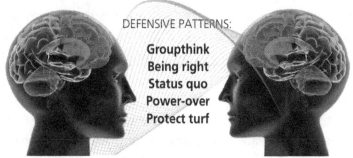

DEFENSIVE PATTERNS:

Groupthink
Being right
Status quo
Power-over
Protect turf

Uncertainty is the fulcrum between distrust and trust.

FIGURE 11–2: At the Moment of Uncertainty

sive routines that are always in people's minds as they come together to do work of any kind, yet they play in the background as the team process unfolds.

This is a superficially comfortable stage because on one level people are "doing work together," but through their avoidance of conflict, real work is not getting done, and they worry about both the work and the relationships that are forming, hence the evolution of the team into the second stage, called storming.

The Storming Stage

In the storming stage, people have low levels of trust; they are often competing with one another. Fear of loss abounds, together with fears about who has power and how to fit in; just below the surface lies fear of how to engage and make a contribution, adding more anxiety to the way people process their experience. In Tuckman's model, every group has a storming stage in which people compete for power and status, for the best ideas, and for position in the in-group.

At the moment of contact, our defensive routines move center stage, influencing the dynamics of the team and focusing the brain toward social protection. People withhold information to make sure they have power, they play their status cards to ensure they have importance, they bond with the right people to make sure they are positioned for success, and they fight to be right so they are perceived as winners in the face of uncertainty.

During this stage, if encouraged to become more open and trusting, people start to put their real issues on the table and become more open to addressing their fears. Unfortunately, in many cases the barriers to trust have become so high that teams and relationships never move past this stage. Often, members of the team will focus on minutiae, micromanage, or take over and assume leadership. At this point, the politics of a team can become a negative driving force and may impede any progress, or even sour the individuals involved and prevent them from opening up to trust in the future.

Many people learn to become conflict averse, to give up and give in, and to turn to passive-aggressive behaviors as a default. This stage can be contentious, unpleasant, and even painful to members of the team who are uncomfortable with conflict. Tolerance of all team members and their differences needs to be emphasized. Without tolerance and patience the team will fail. This phase can become destructive to the team and will decrease motivation if negative behaviors are allowed to get out of control.

The Norming Stage

If the team makes the move into the norming stage they have realized that sharing power and information is necessary for the team to not only survive but thrive. They try to figure out what collaboration means, set rules of engagement, and create team norms. Because they already have a memory of pain and conflict, the team will remember this pain when they are under pressure or are hitting conflicts of opinion or perspective. Once these conflicts take place, they are part of the group memory and group consciousness. Repeats of these conflicts form unhealthy patterns for handling conflict and may persist even when the team moves into more constructive work together.

Depending on how the group interprets what it means to create norms, the norming stage can actually become a process for creating *compliance* rather than for freeing the team to co-create. If the message that norming sends the group is that *it's time to get along and fit in* rather than challenge the group or risk speaking up (something people try to do a lot of during storming), then the norming stage becomes a reinforcement of defensive routines and groupthink, screening out innovation and new ideas.

It's fascinating to see that in both Tuckman's research and other social scientists' research, it's this phase in which many teams lose their creativity. Social norms can stifle healthy dissent, and when team members begin to exhibit groupthink they give up their rights to speak their minds.

In some groups, leaders will need to take a more directorial role to get the team to speak up, and sometimes people will fall back and wait to see what others do rather than risk confrontation. Defensive routines are often just below the surface, and can grip team members' amygdalas at a moment's notice, sending players into silent combat to regain their foothold in the team's hierarchy.

The Performing Stage

The last stage is performing. The goal is for everyone to feel interdependent and for all to work at their peak. Many relationships and groups don't make it to the end of the journey.

While Tuckman's work is brilliant at describing the stages of team development, I have endeavored through my work with Conversational Intelligence to move teams through this process with less "storming" and higher "performing." And building trust through Conversational

Intelligence is the key. When teams focus on building trust early in the process, they become more open, candid, and caring with one another. In other words, they are able to move into Level III early in the process. In addition, by focusing on relationships before they focus on tasks, they become more skillful at handling the difficult conversations and conflicts that often emerge when people launch challenging projects together.

The final outcome is the true test. Those teams who learn to use Conversational Intelligence skills prior to launching a team challenge discover that their level of performance is far beyond what they have experienced in the past. Conversational Intelligence does make a difference!

Finding Our Voice in Team Conversations

"The inner conformist is stronger than the inner activist," said Michael Morris, a psychologist at Columbia University who studies the role of culture in decision making.[1] When we get together with others in a group or team, the power of the group's opinion often exceeds the force of individual voices.

When people join together on teams, the need to belong becomes so powerful that they are often willing to give up what they believe in order to fit in. One study gave a group of students a visual graphic with two sets of lines. It was clear that one line was shorter than the other. Yet when researchers asked each person which line was longer, the subject chose the wrong answer in the experimental group in which the first person to speak up was a dominant voice in the group. The experiment showed that people were willing to give up their own opinions in favor of the group's opinion, even if it was wrong.[2]

Why is this important for understanding Conversational Intelligence? It is because conversations often take place in groups and teams. The need to connect and belong is more powerful than anything else in team dynamics, and people will wait and see what others think before speaking their minds. When they do speak up, they will often modify their "out of the box" thoughts for fear of looking stupid or challenging a group norm.

Overcoming the Fear Factor in Teams

From birth, we learn to avoid physical *pain* and move toward physical *pleasure*. Over time, we learn to protect ourselves from ego pain, building habits that keep us safe from feeling *belittled, embarrassed,* or *devalued*. Within a team, this may translate into avoiding a person who seems to compete with you when you speak up or avoiding a leader who sends you silent signals of disappointment. Pain can also come from what you *anticipate* rather from what is *real*. I call this "feared implications," and it's the hidden and imagined threats that drive us to elevate cortisol levels and weaken our immune systems.

When we live in fear, we withdraw, build our own *story* of reality, imagine others are *out to get us*, and react accordingly. We stop turning to others for help and stop taking feedback from them.

Universal fears include the fear of *being excluded*—so we create networks and exclude others first; *being rejected*—so we reject first; *being judged unfairly*—so we criticize and blame others; *failing*—so we avoid taking risks and making mistakes; *losing power*—so we intimidate others to get power; *feeling stupid*—so we either don't speak up or speak too much; and *looking bad in front of others*—so we save face. When we perceive the world through a lens of fear, our egos drive us to develop patterns of protection. We turn away from others when we are coming from protective behaviors, rather than turning to others for help. Teams that operate from a place of fear and a stance of protection will never be able to move into Level III conversations.

How you manage fear in the workplace determines the levels of productivity and success your team will achieve. As a leader, you can shape the experiences people have at work by reducing fear, shifting an inner focus to an external focus, and creating cultures that facilitate enhanced sensitivity, mutual support, and Conversational Intelligence.

Five Steps to Building TRUST

Following are five ways leaders can eliminate fear within a team using the TRUST Model.

1. **Be present.** Make yourself open to others by being tuned into your relationship environment. People want to connect, and if you are more *Transparent* about what is going on you will send the signal that "we're all in this together." Being present with others enables them to move from "Protect" to "Connect" at the visceral level, the first step to building trust.

2. **Tell people where they stand.** People need to know where they stand so they can let go of their fears and the questions, "Am I good enough?" and "Do I belong?" and can refocus on contributing. Once they know their status in the organization, they often discover that their imagined fears were much worse than reality. Letting people know where they stand builds and strengthens *Relationships.*

3. **Provide context in every communication.** A picture with a frame becomes a different picture. Without background, fear can be elevated by confusion and uncertainty. Context can make things that are bad seem right—or at least far less worrisome. Providing context moves people from uncertainty to *Understanding.*

4. **Catalyze co-creating in conversations.** Frame conversations as dialogues rather than monologues, so people's voices are heard. Create higher levels of engagement and co-creation so people can build a picture of *Shared success,* which diminishes the fear of being lost in the crowd or overshadowed by people with greater status and power.

5. **Use honesty at all times.** No one likes to tell the truth when it will hurt someone or make that person look bad. So we fudge. When the truth surfaces, the impact is twice as bad as it would have been without the fibs. At all times, *Tell the truth*—tactfully and within the appropriate context. Context, in this case, does not mean spin. Don't make a situation sound better than it is, even if you can.

As a leader, you can have no greater resource than a high-performing team. As we apply the wisdom of Conversational Intelligence, we enable people on a team to engage in Level III conversational dynamics and encourage them to speak their minds, leading the whole team to achieve innovative breakthroughs we never thought possible.

Conversational Intelligence in Action

As executive director of the Recreational Software Advisory Council (RSAC), Stephen Balkam was given a prestigious assignment by the German government: to create the conceptual framework for software that would rate and filter material from the Internet that was inappropriate for minors.

Balkam was both nervous and excited about his role, and about what might happen over the first few months of this new engagement. One of his first tasks was to facilitate a RSAC board meeting in Washington, which was convened to shape RSAC's future global strategy.

This meeting would launch a new strategy to develop the first global self-regulatory system for protecting minors from objectionable Internet sites, while at the same time supporting free speech. The organization was about to transform into a global nonprofit—it would change its name from RSAC to ICRA (Internet Content Rating Association). With this change, the organization would elevate its visibility, allowing it to be more effective in creating a framework that rated Internet content and aided parents in filtering potentially harmful sites from their children's searches.

When the self-regulating labeling and filtering components worked together, young children could freely access acceptable programming yet web providers could target their material to appropriate audiences.

What made this "conversation" particularly volatile was that this was a meeting of rivals. Everyone who was anyone in the Internet space was attending the meeting—representatives from AOL, Telecom, Microsoft, and IBM, just to mention a few. Each company wanted to champion free speech, but it also wanted to ensure that those who cared for minors would be able to censor inappropriate material.

Balkam hoped his organization's input would help the ICRA board reshape the mission, redefine the market, and transform the way the organization perceived the system the members were codesigning. But Balkam also knew that each person on the team was bringing a vested interest and his own agenda to the meeting. Each person wanted to make sure the decisions made at the meeting would not harm his own company's business interests. Each wanted to make sure his voice was heard. Each knew his job was to win at all costs on behalf of his business. It was possible that the attendees would not agree on the future direction of ICRA—if so, the meeting would be labeled a failure.

Knowing that in order to achieve his goals, he needed to find a way to get all the attendees to trust both him and one another, Balkam called me to help him with this challenge.

The Backstory

The meeting was going to be rough. I did the pre-interviews and realized how entrenched people were in their points of view. Many were afraid this would not end well even before the meeting started. They were in high levels of "Protect" and "Distrust"—the left side of the ARC of Engagement.

When the meeting started, there was a lot of resistance in the room and high levels of skepticism about whether we could turn a corner on trust. I could tell that people came with their minds made up—this feeling of "foe not friend" is something we all feel when people speak with preconceived outcomes in mind. In meetings, we often see people making suggestions but not listening to others. We see people selling their ideas but not considering the ideas of others. The atmosphere often becomes adversarial and competitive rather than open and candid.

Of course, such groups may make important decisions, but the results usually reflect the ideas people brought to the meeting in the first place. Rather than working in the spirit of new directions and fresh thinking, the group simply plays out variations on old ideas and speaks from participants' original platforms and entrenched points of view.

We made a huge step forward when attendees were transparent about their concerns and even concurred that: "In bad meetings certain individuals try to dominate with their own agendas, while in good meetings everyone harvests new ideas that spring from collaborative, give-and-take discussions."

Good, Bad, and Ugly

At the outset of the ICRA meeting, the group was asked if anyone wished to offer an opinion on what the outcome of the meeting would be. A few people raised their hands and said they were about 70 percent sure about what would happen. They believed the outcome would be deadlock, which signaled that before they could create something new, they had to undo or break through some old thinking and preconceived notions.

Participants then paired up and shared experiences of both great and awful conversations. At the end of this opening exercise, and to the surprise of all twenty-five attendees, the group concluded that they would shun speechmaking and selling in favor of drawing out and experimenting with new ideas. With a flash of insight, the team moved into Level III conversational dynamics right in front of our eyes.

It's one thing to agree to set aside preexisting agendas and instead play with new scenarios; it's another thing to actually make that happen in a roomful of competitors. For some people, just *talking* about new possibilities and scenarios causes visceral reactions, as it did with these twenty-five senior executives, each with vested interests to protect.

For many of us, even talking about something that might take place creates fear about the future outcomes. As we imagine what will happen, our minds are conjuring up a movie of negative consequences. Seeing the possibility of failure in our mind's eye becomes as real as experiencing failure. So many individuals and teams that keep their fears hidden prevent themselves from moving into Level III, while those teams that share and discover both aspirations and threats create a safe space for trust and Level III courage.

Developing a Third Eye about the phenomenon of "phantom fear" is a powerful lesson for teams. We know that talking about change and mentally experiencing change for many of us is the same as actually doing it. For example, let's say we talk about making major changes in a newly merged division or we require people to use a new system that would radically shift how they work together: often, people experience fear and loss right in front of our eyes, even before the change happens.

Fear is a human response to change, and to even simply discussing change. Once we ignite fear of loss we generalize to other fears: fear of conflict, fear of change, fear of failure. And fear is the archenemy of even modest preparation for change, such as scenario building, planning, and testing of new strategies.

Making the Invisible Visible

Visualizing fear and success with others makes the invisible visible. With that in mind, Stephen Balkam started the ICRA meeting by asking participants to literally draw their ideas. On paper, individuals sketched both what the old RSAC system looked like and what the new system could look like. Once the ideas had been captured on flip charts, people drew, resized, combined, and invented new and even more radical scenarios. In other words, Balkam created a safe circle of inclusion where everyone was now thinking together in new ways—drawing rather than talking created a change of mind for all involved.[2]

Participants used colored markers so that they could create overlays to existing diagrams, which they would never have created using words alone. Ideas started to link to other ideas. When the group seemed most stuck, Balkam introduced metaphors and images to inspire them to think in new ways.

Interpreting this experience through the TRUST Model, the team created transparency about their fears of success, identified their thoughts on how the meeting would go, created understanding without fear, and graphically represented what shared success would look like. In taking these steps, the team of potential adversaries shifted from distrust to trust in less than an hour.

Up- and Down-Regulating

The ICRA team had been struggling with how to create a new system architecture that content providers could use in evaluating appropriate material for the web. By the time the session ended, the ICRA board—which started as a group of high-powered competitors—had invented just the innovative architecture they were seeking.

They were able to do this because a space had been opened up to allow trust and a vision of shared success to emerge. The executives learned that by redesigning the agenda to allow for candor and for full disclosure about their fears, they freed themselves to explore ideas they **never before** explored together. The process elevated their bonding and trust, and innovation emerged.

Down-Regulate	Up-Regulate
Fear	Transparency
Power	Relationship building
Uncertainty	Understanding
Being right	Shared vision of success
Groupthink	Truth & empathy

FIGURE 11–3: Up-Regulate/Down-Regulate

The team down-regulated, or minimized, the types of conversations that would trigger fear, power plays, uncertainty, a need to be right, and groupthink, and they up-regulated the types of conversations that inspired transparency, relationship building, understanding, a shared vision of success, and truth and empathy. In other words, together they broke through the barriers to Level III conversations, becoming facilitators and co-creators in Level III.

Removing Barriers to Success

The biggest challenge facing the executives at the ICRA meeting was that they came from different companies, all with their own vested interests. AOL was creating Internet controls for its customers, while Microsoft was creating its own controls. Yet, as members of ICRA, the executives were now being asked to temper their companies' primary interests for the sake of ICRA's interests.

Faced with these challenges, each executive wondered at different points during the meeting, "Whose team am I on anyway?" If the ICRA team developed a global system, would it interfere and compete with what IBM or Microsoft would do with its own content-screening products? How could each executive share and participate without jeopardizing her company's proprietary product information?

One Mind, One Heart

By the time the meeting was over, the executives attending the ICRA meeting came together and felt committed to their shared accountability. While each had come into the meeting to protect his company's interests, by the time the meeting was over the executives had melded together in their intention to come up with a content rating system their companies could subscribe to. They became open to one another, and were able to determine what to share and what not to share to advance the group's best outcomes and also preserve their companies' interests. It was a landmark event for all, and their collective Conversational Intelligence increased.

Takeaways for Your Success

When you join a team, it is your own critical knowledge that makes you unique and valuable. If you share this knowledge or give it away, you need to wonder whether you will lose your unique competitive edge. Do you weaken your power, or is there a way to give power away in order to gain more power?

As you learn how to create more space for trust to grow, you change the conversational landscape. Sometimes you discover you have a bold person inside of you and yet when you speak up, what comes out is less powerful than you'd hoped. You choose words that are not as edgy or ideas that are less profound because you think others will not accept your thoughts or because you don't want to give away what you believe are your vital secrets. So you close up or shrink down your communication to avoid the larger challenge of trusting and sharing. When what you have to say seems to be in conflict with others' opinions, you may step back to protect yourself from harm. Perhaps being bold once cost you some points when you got pushback from an authority figure and you've been gun-shy ever since.

Yet, as the ICRA executives learned, stepping into a conversational space that feels safe and trusting changes everything. Learning to shape the space for trust is core to leadership at all levels in a company—and it is core to human beings of all ages. In our next chapter, we'll explore the Level III practices used by successful leaders and teams undergoing transformational change. How they handled uncertainty through co-creating conversations profoundly changed the future of their organizations!

12

Changing the Game Through Conversational Intelligence

If you want to build a ship, don't drum up people together to collect wood, and don't assign them tasks and work but rather teach them to long for the endless immensity of the sea.

—ANTOINE DE SAINT-EXUPERY

When we are frightened by change, our brains fall back into protective behaviors. It's as though all our instinctual networks know how to ensure we are not harmed. Millions of years of evolution have ensured we don't lose that exquisite capacity to protect our genes, our families and communities, and our future.

Not all change evokes fear. When I was sixteen I was selected to be part of the Experiment in International Living, an amazing organization started by Dr. Donald Watt. Today the Experiment is still thriving, and it enables thousands of teenagers to live in countries with other families—to become immersed in another culture, learn another language, and then to become ambassadors of change in the world. This is where I learned how to transform my thinking about change. Our slogan was "Expect the Unexpected!" This one phrase shifted my thinking. I learned to reframe change from fear to curiosity. From that moment forward I saw change as an opportunity to go on a journey of discovery and learn about new things, expand my world, expand my friendships, and make a difference.

Yet, when I ask leaders their reaction to the word "change," most say two things almost instantly: "failure and loss." I found this really fascinating and dug into writings, stories, and interviews from my archives of research with clients and in the media, and discovered that more people associated change with loss than with discovery. More people saw change as an enemy rather than as a friend. My early experiences as a Global Teen Leader developed my aptitude for conversational agility— an ability to reframe and revise my thinking and to see change as a positive growth experience. This powerful phrase, "Expect the Unexpected," enabled me to change the conversation in my head, and also to change the course of my own history, leading me to want to understand how conversations change our reality—now and into the future.[1]

Seeing Change with New Eyes

Change can be a door to a new future or can anchor us to the past. Many of us bring our history with us during change, and when this happens we become anchored in old thinking rather than free to think in new ways. When we learn to apply Conversational Intelligence practices and spend more time in Level III interaction dynamics and conversational rituals, we actually *instruct our brains* how to master, navigate, and drive change as a natural way of life.

When I put my **organizational anthropologist** hat on, I'm able to think and speak clearly about change. It's when I'm in this mind-set that I see and appreciate the power of conversation to shape our humanity. Looking back into history and exploring how ancient civilizations have handled change, we learn a core principle behind the power of Conversational Intelligence. Human beings have become masters of creating conversational rituals to help us master change. Anytime our lives are disrupted by change, we turn to conversational rituals to "re-anchor" us to a safe place.

When we are facing challenges in our lives and we are fearful, we may pray to God for help. Prayer is a ritual. When a football team is facing challenges on the field, they go into a huddle and chant some special words important to them and say, "Go team!" This anchors them to a place of shared success so they can face the challenges to come. Take a minute and think about the rituals that enable you to become grounded again in the face of change. Do you call someone you trust and talk it out? Do you write up a plan to get refocused? Do you eat peanut butter because it makes you feel comfortable? Do you reach out and connect or do you pull into your own "cave" and reflect?

Change disturbs our predictable patterns. If I do things the same way every day, and every day it works, I want to repeat what I've done so I know the outcome. I can feel safe, and when I feel safe, my levels of cortisol are lower and my mind is open to explore, discover, and learn without feeling I will make mistakes that may damage my ego or reputation or, even more critically, my confidence in myself.

Change brings with it risks. In the Wikipedia entry on "risk," the definition includes: *the potential that a chosen action or activity (including the choice of inaction) will lead to a loss (an undesirable outcome). No change—no risk.* When I *limit or minimize the fear* associated with risk of failure I am increasing my chances for success. Conversational Intelligence gives us the ability to reframe, refocus, and redirect our thinking, and therefore change the way we navigate the risks and challenges of our lives. Learning to use our conversational skills brings greater mastery over both our inner spaces (our intention) and our outer spaces (the impact). Aligning intention and impact is a core C-IQ skill, and one that is worth practicing and succeeding in.

Success is brain food, a reward for doing something right. The incredible neurotransmitters associated with success are highly reinforcing of taking risks, learning new things, experimenting, and feeling good about ourselves in the future.

Neuroscience is showing that our brains like certainty and predictability. In fact, when we attempt to predict the future, and we are right about our predictions, we become more confident in taking risks even in the face of loss. By applying our conversational agility skills of *reframing* to the challenges of change, we are *giving new meaning* to mistakes and labeling them as experiments. Experiments exist on the right side of the Conversational Dashboard. As we move to the right, we free our brains to *choose risk* rather than be fearful that risk will always lead to loss.

Conversational Intelligence and Change

When successful change occurs, those involved feel like the authors of change rather than the objects of change. They feel fully invested, accountable, and energetic about the future, even in the face of huge challenges. Despite good intentions, many old approaches to change have failed to help organizations really make desired changes stick, or to become part of the organizational DNA. I have asked myself why a thousand times, and have come to some clarity on what blocks change and what to do about it.

Many leaders, without realizing it, apply Level I or Level II interaction dynamics in moving organizations through change. They decide where they want people to go and communicate the plan using a top-down, command-and-control approach. Their well-intentioned efforts to get everyone on the same page, delivers the wrong energy for "moving" an organization toward transformation and change. However, when leaders help create a framework for change and then stimulate Level III interaction dynamics, they are catalyzing change within the framework rather than dictating the way change needs to happen.

This shift toward "setting the framework" and enabling Level III interaction dynamics is new for many leaders. What we often see in failed attempts at transformation is that, after much effort and lots of marching to a new drum, organizations give up. Some even find that people are more despondent and disappointed than they were before the failed transformation effort.

The keys to successful change lie in understanding change from a Conversational Intelligence perspective. Change is more a process that "we" do together than one that "I" do alone. When leaders honor and respect how our WE-centric brains respond to change, they will become champions of a new level of leadership fueled by applying all three levels of Conversational Intelligence at the right time and in the right way.

Creating the Space for a New Picture of Reality

Conversational Intelligence gives us tools for letting go of the past and transforming the future. Recently, I worked with a prestigious museum known for its innovative approach to displaying art. Many museums organize exhibits by time period or by geographic society: all Egyptian art is placed together, all African, all Asian, and so on. The museum has become known for its unusual approach to organizing art so that higher-level insights emerge about humanity and the role art plays in the story of our human evolution. For example, the museum created an exhibition called the *Blue Exhibit*, which looked at how and why the color blue was used across the world at a specific time in history.

The museum has a team of more than eighteen curators, each one responsible for his or her own collections. According to its strategic plan, the museum proposed a new, centrally located section to house themed collections in which different curators could showcase a combined collection. Conflicts over what, how, and who would be part of this showcase continued for more than a year, with no decision reached on how to share the space.

The curators felt that if they gave their best art pieces to the joint display, their individual collections would suffer. There was a lot of conversation about what themes might work, but these discussions yielded little positive outcome. Over time, there was a lot of positioning, with more talk about what it meant to "lose a good piece from a collection" than talk of creating something great together. In Conversational Intelligence terms, the conversations amongst the curators had become stuck in Level II. Curators were feeling that change was about loss—the most common emotion associated with change. They also felt that by giving up something they valued as the best in their collection, that they would diminish the value of their individual collections, which were housed throughout the museum. Curators became entrenched in their positional perspectives; they were advocating for their points of view and were not open to seeing the bigger picture. They needed to tap into the possibilities of Level III—the level at which everyone's mind becomes *open to discovering a new reality*. The fear of loss was holding the curators back from moving into "Share and Discover" interaction dynamics.

Creating the Space for Co-Creation

In preparing the curators for our conversational journey—learning to step from Level I into Levels II and III transformational conversations—I did a process called "speed interviews." I set up fifteen-minute meetings with each of the curators to gather the fears and aspirations of those attending the team meeting. Each person put their fears on the table, and in the process moved from suppressing the fear to expressing it.

Without teaching it explicitly, I was consciously modeling Level III conversational dynamics. I was also using the Conversational Intelligence TRUST Model with them, starting with "Transparency."

As each person became transparent about their aspirations and intentions to co-create and also what was threatening their—their fears and "stories" about what was going on—they "felt a release inside." This process gave the curators the courage and a space to share their realities without judgment. They could speak out and have a voice, and not be judged for how they were feeling. Each person felt that they had a

POWER & INFLUENCE

	INTERACTION DYNAMICS	IMPACT
LEVEL I TELL ASK	**"TELL & ASK"** *Telling what is on your mind (I-centric)*	**TRANSACTIONAL INFLUENCE** *Influence through information sharing*
LEVEL II FINITE ADVOCATE INQUIRE	**"ADVOCATE & INQUIRE"** *Influence others to your position*	**POSITIONAL INFLUENCE** *Influence through personal or positional power*
LEVEL III INFINITE SHARE DISCOVER	**"SHARE & DISCOVER"** *Releasing energy to co-create influence*	**TRANSFORMATIONAL INFLUENCE** *Influence through energy shifting*

FIGURE 12-1: Power and Influence

chance to speak out and have their opinions valued. The interview process was setting the stage for Level III interaction dynamics, and setting rules of engagement, which would take place when all the curators got together.

As it turned out, all eighteen people had the same fear: that using strong pieces from their individual collections in the "museum event" would weaken their own displays. This common fear, I knew, would create a bonding moment among the curators. The next phase was to bring the team together so they could start to reveal their inner thoughts and feelings to one another—to work on Transparency + Relationship together.

During the meeting, the team talked about what was bothering them, and also about what they aspired to create. They learned they could move from a state of *protection* to *partnering* with others by being open to *sharing and discovering* their fears and aspirations. In a team exercise, the curators also shared, "What I respect about you and what I need from you." This enabled them to recognize the strengths in others and to prime one another for partnering and co-creating to take place. It also built a higher level of *understanding* than they had ever had before. They worked through the TRUST Model to create openness, bonding, connectivity, and empathy for one another. By stepping into one another's shoes and listening without judgment, the curators were triggering the prefrontal cortex (the executive brain) to access higher-level capacities, including how to handle gaps between reality and aspirations; how to access new thinking; and how to move into infinite thinking together and co-create new possibilities. Without this part of the brain activated, we fall back into positional thinking and fight for our vested interests.

The team lived in Level III dynamics during our time together. They were more candid and caring than they had ever been before, and they spoke truth without triggering deep fear. They stayed in high levels of trust. The created the space for *shared success*.

Then a breakthrough occurred. As people stayed open to the possibility that they might discover ideas they had never thought of before, a *new word* emerged in their conversation, and this new word created a whole shift in the interaction dynamic. The eighteen curators discovered or, better yet, co-created the concept of "pods." This was a way of describing the space where they could do experiments together. They envisioned how pods all over the museum could house artifacts that showed links between different time periods, different geographies, and other themes they would co-create. Soon the group had three to five possible pods for displaying their artwork together.

Prior to this Co-creating Conversation, the group had been arguing about what to give up for the greater good, and this stimulated fear responses. They were stuck in Level II positional conversations and were getting nowhere. After the experience of living in Level III conversations together, the group became more comfortable with transparency, candor, and truth telling, and at the same time became more open to sharing and supporting one another. Most surprising to all was that to achieve a breakthrough, they needed to co-create and define a new term they had never used before. It was a group aha moment that opened up a whole new way of organizing their work to benefit the museum's visitors. This created a bonding experience (oxytocin rush), which started to open up new conversations about "what ifs." They imagined new things they could do together, fostering a higher level of risk taking and openness than they had experienced in years.

Co-creating new terms is a high Level III skill. I see it in every major transformation I do with clients, and I teach it in all my Conversational Intelligence workshops, presentations, and summits. Co-creating new terms opens the "infinite space" our minds need to be free to connect with others in new ways. By co-creating a definition we ensure that we all mean the same thing and that it's what we want the term to mean. And when people are uncertain about what the new term means, they test assumptions with each other rather than allowing themselves to "make stuff up!"

Interpretations, drama, and negative storytelling give way to a sense of shared success and bonding that is evergreen in shaping the new relationships of the team. The director of the museum was so awed by this moment in the team's evolution that he wanted to save all of the flip charts so they could remember the conversational journey and the powerful breakthroughs they had experienced together.

Getting Unstuck from Level II

In the 1990s, Lockheed Martin was organized around business units. The corporation wanted to put in an ERP (enterprise resource planning) system for all divisions to use, but there was great resistance. Each division had its own legacy system in place and was comfortable using it.

The company had five divisions at the time, and each president had done an extraordinary job of developing and streamlining systems so that he had control over his bottom- and top-line growth. Bringing in an enterprise-wide system was threatening to the leaders. As one described, "It takes a long time to develop an ERP system for the whole company that will also reflect the needs of each division. From what I can see, I'll need to give up features that I need in my division for the benefit of the whole system—and I won't be able to guarantee my revenue projections. It's just not going to work for me."

Conversations ensued at all levels of the company. People were strongly entrenched in their division's current state, and there was deadlock. They were in Level II positional dynamics, and each president and his direct reports were building their cases and sharpening their positions. As weeks passed, the company took steps to name an authority who would make the decisions and move the presidents into agreement. It assigned a VP to head the ERP project, and IBM helped map out the system-wide program. There was a lot of conflict over transitioning to the new system, and as a result, the company discovered it was burning $1 million dollars a day due to indecision. People were not on board, and in meeting after meeting the executives attempted to work through the issues with no luck.

Divisional heads and their direct reports all had a vested interest in their own approach. They could outline the ways a change would jeopardize their bottom lines. At meetings to discuss the new ERP system, each executive was prepared with facts and data to try to convince others his way was the right way. Politicking was taking place behind the scenes in an attempt to influence others. There was no clear consensus or a road map showing how to get there.

Over a two-week period, I architected a new pathway for co-creating the decision—and it changed everything. First, I shaped the conversational space for Level III interaction dynamics. To prime the executives for opening to the larger enterprise issues and to help them see how to get from self-interest to shared success, I worked with a senior team of executives to design the meeting space. We arranged for a large room and hung it with visual materials that provided background on the intentions and outcomes behind the proposed ERP system.

Then we convened a meeting of the top sixty-five executives, and I facilitated the conversations by stepping them into the Level III framework. Around the room I posted the concepts that elevate our minds to Level III. First we talked about where they were in the decision process (making the journey, aspirations, and threats transparent). They talked about the "The Ladder of Conclusions." We talked about how, when we interact with others from an entrenched point of view, our conversations trigger neurochemistry that influences the way we make decisions. With high levels of cortisol, we close down our listening and learning brains and communicate from a position of entrenchment. We also go up the ladder and make assumptions, interpretations, and conclusions about others, often labeling them foe rather than friend.

During the meeting I shared the science behind the Ladder of Conclusions and helped them see how states of mind determine outcomes. I shared that they were likely not open to influence given their current state. Then I talked about how to create leadershifts—and how to use discovery questions and Level III strategies to leave persuading behind. Posting the Conversational Dashboard as a visual, along with the Ladder of Conclusions, helped them visualize the conversational space and the conversational journey they were about to travel together. We talked about rules of engagement and what makes a great conversation. Then the room of sixty-five entrenched executives had a Level III conversation for ninety minutes.

Within ninety minutes, these key leaders agreed to move forward. They spent almost the whole time listening to one another and learning about other perspectives. They stayed open to being influenced.

Prior to the priming process, the leaders were advocating their own perspectives and were not open to influence. They were in a win-at-all-costs mind-set and didn't want to give in. Fear of losing revenues by adopting the new company-wide ERP system prevented them from experimenting together with options that would work better for everyone. Once they became open to sharing proprietary information and exploring different avenues for creating an outcome that worked well for everyone, new ideas emerged.

Rewiring Level III into Everyday Life

We started, at the beginning of this book, with a quote that has been the framework for all of the work I do with clients, and I'd like to end with it as well. It's been my inspiration through every project, every transformation, and every relationship:

> To get to the next level of greatness depends on the quality of the culture, which depends on the quality of relationships, which depends on the quality of conversations. Everything happens through conversation.

By learning to graft new conversational rituals into your interaction dynamics, you will discover new doors opening up in your mind and in your reality.

Following are four conversational rituals and success strategies[2] that will trigger the natural ability for change to evolve; change is hardwired into your DNA. These rituals will enable you to become a facilitator of change and a master of Conversational Intelligence.

Identify the success strategies you are using, and decide which ones you want to use more often to expand your effectiveness as a leader:

1. See Resistance in a New Light

Resistance and *skepticism* are companions to change. It's almost impossible to ask people to do things differently without them pushing back and seeking to understand the implications of the change on their lives. If we block questions or do not deal with them, we turn up the level of protection within our people and raise our perceived need to push harder. Yet too often we interpret the pushback as *no* and we respond by trying to sell people on why change is good. When *tell* or *sell* doesn't work we resort to *yell*, which can take the form of actual yelling at those who seem resistant, or we can turn to others to influence our target resisters. Either way, we are not dealing with resistance productively or constructively. We are, in fact, fanning the flame of resistance and fear.

Reframe: *To put Conversational Intelligence to work, stop thinking of your job as managing resistance and instead accept resistance as a natural part of change. People need to challenge new ideas before they can accept them. For full ownership and accountability to take place, people need to be in the conversation about how to change rather than being asked to merely comply. When leaders reframe in this way, they see that conversations release new energy for change—which will propel their efforts forward faster.*

---

2. Welcome and Facilitate Conversations

We underestimate the amount of dialogue and conversations people need to feel comfortable and to understand what changes are being required, suggested, or proposed. When people are afraid, they listen differently—they listen for the *implications* of how change will negatively impact them. While these may not be openly discussed, each person is having her own internal dialogue hypothesizing what these changes might be; most often there is a huge fear of loss and rarely an anticipation of gain. People fear that through change they will be rejected, moved to lower positions, or asked to *leave the company*. The *need to belong is strong*. Everyone wants to be part of the winning team.

Social neuroscientists now believe that the need to belong trumps the need for safety. They say that we are social beings, and being part of a group is so hardwired into us that it drives everything that has to do with culture and organization. When we feel rejected we react with more fear and resistance. When we feel we are part of the solution we find our place in supporting the solution.

Changing mind-sets: *To put Conversational Intelligence to work, create forums where people can have open, candid conversations and learn what is going on and where they belong in the newly emerging order. Transparency and openness have a facilitative impact, transforming fears into constructive strategies for success. Putting the feared implications on the table and facilitating open discussions and conversations about what's in it for them and why and how changes are taking place, helps people shift their mind-sets from loss to gain, from fear to hope, and from scarcity to abundance.*

---

3. Engage Head, Heart, and Spirit

People are emotional during times of change. Too often we fall into the trap of thinking that if we give employees the facts and explain why change needs to take place from an economic point of view, they'll *buy into the change.* We overestimate *the power of logic* and underestimate *the power of storytelling,* an appeal to belonging and the positive emotions of belonging.

Storytelling: *To put Conversational Intelligence to work, use storytelling—narrative that engages people's emotions and creativity—to make change happen. Storytelling triggers the head, heart, and spirit and causes us to bond rather than fight. Oxytocin is a hormone that causes us to bond with others in times of stress and*

---

change. Positive and uplifting storytelling increases the oxytocin level, which creates uplifting and positive outcomes from the ensuing conversations. The fearful "I" becomes "WE." When this happens, individuals become a strong team poised to work together to create change rather than be the objects of change. Narratives and stories help unite all heads, hearts, and spirits, enabling a shared perspective and new set of possibilities for the future.

4. Create the Space for Change

Too often, we want change to happen *fast and without pain.* We want to inject a serum that makes the pain and conflict go away. Many of us avoid conflict for fear of losing our relationships with others, and research shows we may even give up our beliefs to ensure we stay in sync with others. This can look like premature agreement or, in some cases, forced consensus. In an attempt to gain consensus we may push forward into agreement without really vetting divergent ideas, and in fact eclipsing the new and innovative thinking that could emerge.

We have likely all been part of change management programs that end with a new set of policies being disseminated to the organization with the belief that a new dictum will "zap" the culture and create change overnight. This is an example of using Level I transactional "selling" or Level II positional influence to move an organization through change. Proclamations and policy changes on paper will not create the fundamental changes to DNA that organizations need to catalyze change. Use Conversational Intelligence skills to create change is where true organic transformation lies.

Co-creating Conversations. *To put your Conversational Intelligence to work, create conversational practices that enable you to work on co-creating the future. These conversations are* *not about a quick fix or a new policy. This is not about lecturing or tell–sell–yell but about practicing navigating with others in and out of scenarios from many perspectives. Such an approach lets us arrive at practices and rituals for how work gets done inside our culture that we all embrace. These conversations allow us to create a movie screen on which to project scenarios for the future so we can explore and choose the best paths. We gain an understanding of others' perspectives, enabling us to form a WE-centric rather than an I-centric view of the future. Change leaders must learn to create the conversational space for change, to reduce fears and threats, and to help people find their place in the change process. When this happens, we breathe in a coherent rather than a fearful way. To breathe means to aspire. When we are calm and connected to others during change, our aspirations become greater and our capabilities increase.*

Conversations connect us and bring us into communion with others. Without conversations, our ability to evolve, develop, and innovate drastically diminishes. For this reason, mastering our moments of contact is the art of great leadership—it's the art of great negotiators, great leaders, great actors, great writers, and great human beings. When we learn to notice patterns and how to influence them, and when we learn to notice what happens in the moment and how to shape moments for impact, we are using the skills of Conversational Intelligence. We learn to redirect, reframe, revise, restate, refocus, and reengage...and to apply all of our "change skills" in the moment.

Everyone can become a master of Conversational Intelligence. We don't need to be visionaries, or to have the top seven attributes of great leaders. We don't need to be born on the right day or have someone give us a million dollars. We don't need to have attended Harvard or been born into a distinguished family. Conversational Intelligence teaches us to see differently—to listen differently—and to process what we are perceiving differently. When we do that, we act in the moment in ways that create energy, activate energy, and help guide energy toward more productive and more powerful ends with others.

EPILOGUE

Creating Conversations
That Transform the World

I grew up in a unique family. When I was eleven, my parents took us to Mexico, and my sister, brother, and I spent the summer at a Mexican International Camp, Instituto Americano. Living for a summer with youth from around the world, whose native languages were all different, was initially a huge challenge for an eleven-year-old. Yet we found a common bridge—we learned to speak Spanish together. This was a transformational experience for me, and it taught me how to *connect with others* through broader dimensions than words alone. The work I do today would not have happened were it not for this incredible life-changing experience. What took us to Mexico was an even more fascinating story.

My father was a dentist, and he had an idea that seemed impossible to many. He went to the State Department and proposed his outrageous idea, and it became a reality. My father was a very innovative dentist, inventing tools and new practices in his field. He taught at Temple Dental School in addition to having his own practice. But that was not enough. My father said to the State Department: "I would like to bring dentistry around the world."

When he returned from his visit to Washington, he told us he was going to be the first dental ambassador from the United States, and he was going to travel around the world teaching "his dentistry." Spending the summer at Instituto Americano was our firsthand experience of what this meant. Over the years, my father taught himself seven languages, and he and my mother—his dental hygienist and the love of his life—visited more than eighteen countries, where they lectured and taught and created a bridge from the United States to other countries, other leaders, and other cultures.

Conversations That Shape Our History

When my father was young he was a stutterer. He stuttered his way through elementary school and high school. While he was outrageously smart, he was unable to speak well and was teased unmercifully. Teasing created more stuttering, and it was hard for him to build deep friendships.

Then a miracle happened. He had a teacher who changed his life. Much like the speech tutor depicted in *The King's Speech*, my father's teacher had conversations with him in a way no one else had. She made him feel whole and, although he had a serious stutter, through her conversations with him, he found the courage to take on the lead role in the school play. Somehow, her confidence in him and her caring ways changed his life. Because of his lead role in the school play, his stuttering disappeared.

There is much research about the neuroscience of brain plasticity, about how we shape and reshape our identities, and about the complexity of speech and stuttering. Research indicates that as we grow and learn new things, we allocate new space in our brains to learning. The phenomenal plasticity of our brains allows us to create new personas, identities, and competencies. Because of this teacher's special relationship with my father, and because of the powerful and transformational conversations they had together, the path his life would take was forever changed.

My dad went on to become the head of the debating team in college and the valedictorian of his class. He did fulfill his dream of bringing dentistry around the world, and when he visited each country, he gave presentations and keynotes in the native language.

My exposure to many different cultures at a young age undoubtedly influenced my own trajectory, and the power of conversation has always been a subject of great interest to me. In college, I pursued interdisciplinary studies at Temple University including biochemistry, linguistics, anthropology, archeology, psychology, and general semantics. Later, I studied in programs on human behavior, organizational behavior, and corporate and political communications at Drexel University, Harvard University, and Fairfield University. No program *alone* could give me answers to my big questions, and my work became my experimental laboratory for figuring out how conversations transform history.

Conversations That Transform History

Through my work as a consultant and coach and my years of research and experience, I have come to understand that conversations can transform who we are, our relationships, our work environments, and our ability to succeed. As we apply Conversational Intelligence to our interactions, we can change our personal trajectory; on a much grander scale, conversations have the ability to change the history of nations and peoples.

My quest for understanding conversations has taken on a new energy over the past decade, as my work has turned more global and my interests have expanded. I was part of a small group of people who launched the We Are Family Foundation (WAFF).[1] Our vision is to foster a global community by creating and supporting programs that inspire and educate the next generation about respect, understanding, and cultural diversity, while simultaneously striving to solve some of our biggest global programs. Our most important initiative is called Three Dot Dash.[2] Three Dot Dash® is a global initiative of WAFF that supports Global Teen Leaders (GTLs) who are actively working on projects that promote a more peaceful society by addressing basic human needs—food, water, health, shelter, safety, education, and the environment. We have also launched TEDxTeen, a yearly forum bringing together inspiring teens to share their stories about changing the world.[3] Our TEDxTeens are taking on global challenges and inventing cures for what we thought were incurable diseases; they are finding new diagnostics for making early identification of other diseases; and they are bringing messages about how to create peace around the globe.[4]

In addition to being a board member of WAFF, I was invited to be on the board of Expeditionary Learning, now called EL Education. This extraordinary educational organization was originally launched by professors from Harvard who invented the Outward Bound program; EL was spun off into its own educational movement and since then has grown to more than 160 schools in the U.S. EL Education was awarded a contract to develop the core curriculum in New York State, enabling other schools to draw from its advanced and conversationally intelligent approach for educating our children in K–8 schools. I am proud of EL Education's work, which represents the most engaging, affirming, and challenging ways to teach children to develop both character and intelligence that I've ever seen. In addition to its profound practices for advancing education in the U.S., their program embodies an outstanding example of the application of Conversational Intelligence in education.

Our commitment to building a stronger, more communicative, and healthier world is deeply focused on educating leaders to learn and embrace Conversational Intelligence in the workplace. From the day employees join a company, they can learn Conversational Intelligence (C-IQ) frameworks, philosophies, and wisdom; in doing so, they set a foundation for mutual success throughout the company—globally. We are immersed in helping companies with workforces as large as hundreds of thousands and as small as one hundred learn how to "graft" Conversational Intelligence into the culture. We are certifying consultants and coaches in different countries who are also going on to certify others inside of companies. We have partnered with incredible consultants in places such at the U.K., Benelux, South Africa, Finland, Kenya, South America, Mexico, India, Guatemala, Argentina, and Australia to launch Creating WE Institutes globally and serve as our Centers of Excellence in their countries. These partners are a growing part of who we are becoming (http://www.creatingwe.com/institute/global-institutes).

In 2014 I was asked to speak at WBECS (World Business Executive Coaching Summit)—along with 50 other thought leaders—through webinars, which were listened to by more than twenty thousand coaches globally during the course of 2014 and 2015. My sessions were the highest rated, and as a result, WBECS and I moved forward to launch the first-of-its-kind Conversational Intelligence for Coaches program, that will touch coaches in every part of the world.

During this critical time in our history, we are searching for new ways to engage, lead, govern, and make critical decisions. Throughout this book, you have explored the neuroscience behind conversations, learned to identify Level I, II, and III Conversational Dynamics, and started on your personal path to increased Conversational Intelligence. I sincerely hope you will become a part of a strong conversational community, dedicated to opening understanding and changing our world for the better.

Moving forward, my vision is to forge relationships with those working in other neuroscience practice areas to explore the dynamics of conversations and how our brain, mind, and heart is impacted when we are engaged in conversation. When our body senses a conversational threat—what happens in the moment, and what is the ripple effect? Our research and experiments within companies will go beyond what happens to one person when conversational threats emerge and will look more deeply into how we, human beings, can learn the conversational rituals that activate our empathy networks. All humans—from young children to adults—can learn to develop conversational habits and patterns that create healthy environments. Through C-IQ, we now have to tools to learn and practice how to shape conversations, and conversational spaces that will create a world with more compassion than threat, and more foresight and insight than fear and judgment.

My vision is to bring Conversational Intelligence into business, education, and government—as well as other places where healthy conversations can drive success. Being able to help others elevate the quality of our relationships through healthier conversations in every part of our lives is a mission I think about every day and every minute of my life. I think about this focus intensely, and now I have found partners around the world who are becoming as mesmerized by this topic as I am—I am not alone anymore—and that's a great, great feeling!

ENDNOTES

Introduction

1. Reality gaps: Each of us maps reality differently. Reality includes both current reality and what we envision the future to be—our aspirations. When our perspectives differ, gaps emerge and can be perceived as conflicts. Learning how to identify and narrow the gaps raises our C-IQ.

2. Guy Boulton, "Researchers: Severe Poverty Affects Brain Size," *Milwaukee Journal Sentinel*, September 13, 2015, http://www.thonline.com/news/business/article _565fff88-8174-5f01-8c06-de758514b592.html. The UW–Madison study was led by Barbara Wolfe and Seth Pollak, a professor of psychology and director of the Child Emotion Lab. Two former graduate students were also involved in the study and served as coauthors of the recent article: Nicole Hair, an economist now at the University of Michigan, and Jamie Hanson, a psychologist and neuroscientist now at Duke University.

3. Nicole L. Hair; Jamie L. Hanson; Barbara L. Wolfe; Seth D. Pollak, "Association of Child Poverty, Brain Development, and Academic Achievement", *JAMA Pediatrics*, September 2015, Vol 169, No. 9.

4. I wrote this thirty years ago to frame the work I do with organizations.

5. http://www.inc.com/thomas-koulopoulos/5-of-the-biggest-trends-for-2016 -that-you-probably-haven-t-even-heard-of.html

6. http://blogs.microsoft.com/blog/2016/04/01/build-2016-conversational -intelligence-new-innovations-for-windows-10-and-cloud-tools-for-all -developers-weekend-reading-april-1-edition/#sm.0000u9kl099rgdgxxm61139 zlwa9m

Chapter 1

1. Caroline Williams, "Are These the Brain Cells That Gave Us Consciousness?," *New Scientist*, July 23, 2012.

2. John Allman, et al, "The von Economo Neurons in the Frontoinsular and Anterior Cingulate Cortex," *Annals of the New York Academy of Sciences*, 1225, (2011): 59.; California Institute of Technology in Pasadena.

3. Jack Hitt, "Words on Trial," New Yorker, July 23, 2012, 24.

4. Adam Grant, *Give and Take: A Revolutionary Approach to Success* (New York: Viking Press, 2013).

5. See interview on CBS, "Addicted to Being Right," at www.creatingwe.com

Chapter 2

1. Ming Hsu et al, "Neural Systems Responding to Degrees of Uncertainty in Human Decision-Making," *Science*, Vol. 310, no. 5754, 1680–1683, (December 9, 2005)

2. Rollin McCraty and Doc Childre, "Coherence: Bridging Personal, Social, and Global Health," *Alternative Therapies* 6, no. 4 (2010).

Chapter 3

1. Richard S. Tedlow, *Denial: Why Business Leaders Fail to Look Facts in the Face—and What to Do About It* (New York: Portfolio, 2010).

Chapter 4

1. Neuroscientists describe the uniqueness of each person's neural patterns as neural diversity.

Chapter 5

1. HeartMath Institute is one of the originators of the Heart Breathing techniques used to bring our hearts back into a coherent rhythm, a practice that also has a positive impact on calming the amygdala and enabling higher levels of problem solving and innovative thinking.

2. When producers edit a motion picture, one reel becomes the "master" and all of the footage from other reels captured during movie making are called the "slaves."

3. The brain's ability to reorganize itself by forming new neural connections throughout life. Neuroplasticity allows the neurons (nerve cells) in the brain to

compensate for injury and disease and to adjust their activities in response to new situations or to changes in their environment.

4. An enormous amount of neuroscientific research has been done on positive emotions. Dr. Martin Seligman, from the University of Pennsylvania, created a field called Positive Psychology and launched a huge movement globally.

Chapter 6

I. H. Mercier and H. Landemore, "Reasoning Is for Arguing; Understanding the Successes and Failures of Deliberation," Political Psychology, 2012.

Chapter 8

I. Rollin McCraty and Bob Marrios-Choplin, Institute of HeartMath, 1998.

Chapter 10

I. Leon Neyfakh, "How to Change a Culture," *Boston Globe*, September 23, 2012.

Chapter 11

I. Influence: Most people change their opinions to coincide with those of experts or bosses, a phenomenon known as "agreement with experts." Researchers also found that most participants were likely to increase their positive opinion of a song if the experts also liked it, and lower their rating of a song if the experts didn't like it. This shift in opinion was reflected in ventral striatum activity. Source: Wellcome Trust Centre for Neuroimaging at University College, London, England, June 2009.

2. The visual cortex makes up 60 percent of the human brain.

Chapter 12

I. Inspired by an article I wrote with Joe Bonito, a long-time friend and colleague.

Epilogue

I. For more information about the We Are Family Foundation, visit wearefamilyfoundation.org.

2. For more information on Three Dot Dash visit http://www.threedotdash.org/

3. For more information about TEDxTEEN, visit www.wearefamilyfoundation.org/what-we-do/tedxteen

4. http://tedxteen.com/talks/tedxteen-2016-london

REFERENCES

Allman, John, et al. "The von Economo Neurons in the Frontoinsular and Anterior Cingulate Cortex." *Annals of the New York Academy of Sciences* 1225 (2011).

Grant, Adam. *Give and Take: A Revolutionary Approach to Success.* New York: Viking Press, 2013.

Hitt, Jack. "Words on Trial." *New Yorker*, July 23, 2012.

Science 9 December 2005: Vol. 310 no. 5754 pp. 1680–1683

McCraty, Rollin, and Doc Childre. "Coherence: Bridging Personal, Social, and Global Health." *Alternative Therapies* 6, no. 4 (2010).

McCraty, Rollin, and Bob Marrios-Choplin. Institute of HeartMath, 1998.

Mercier, H., and H. Landemore. "Reasoning Is for Arguing; Understanding the Successes and Failures of Deliberation." *Political Psychology*, 2012.

Neyfakh, Leon. "How to Change a Culture." *Boston Sunday Globe*, September 23, 2012.

Tedlow, Richard S. *Denial: Why Business Leaders Fail to Look Facts in the Face—and What to Do About It.* New York: Portfolio, 2010.

Williams, Caroline. "Are These the Brain Cells That Gave Us Consciousness?" *New Scientist*, July 23, 2012.

ACKNOWLEDGMENTS

Trust is the foundation of our humanity, and the fuel for navigating and creating the future - *trust changes reality....*

Conversational Intelligence would not have been possible without the help of a very supportive group of people who I'd like to acknowledge.

My agent, *Al Zuckerman, CEO of Writer's House,* who stayed with me on this project through many iterations of proposals and frameworks while I was sorting out the connection between Conversational Intelligence and trust. Through his tenacity at not letting these ideas blow in the wind, he found my valued publisher, Bibliomotion, specifically Jill Friedlander, Erika Heilman, who got the concept, and the potential that this book has in catalyzing Level III Co-creating Conversations®, which catalyze and facilitate how people do good work together in the world.

Next are my valued colleagues—Roxanne Panero who worked so diligently with me to illustrate Conversational Intelligence—for this book and for all the materials we have generated over the past ten years; Brian Penry, of Penry Creative, who helped give a face to our Creating WE Institute and who has worked with me for twenty-five years to put energy into bringing my evolving ideas to life through his creative graphic renderings; Lynn and Michael Bud, of Square Squared, who have fashioned the Creating WE presence on www.conversationalintelligence.com and www.creatingwe.com; and to Michelle Boos-Stone who, for over the past two decades, has been my trusted graphic recorder and collaborator for many of our Conversational Intelligence Summits. Another very special thanks to Bobbi Benson, who has worked with me to create our Conversational Intelligence mini-books and Neuro-tip Series, as well as our interns and researchers over the past years: Mrin Patil, Carla Rood, Missy Reilly, Brian Frederickson, MA, Rami Glatt, and Yaakov Cohen.

Next, to Ken Shelton, editor of Executive Excellence, who gave me my first big break in writing when he published my article on Vital Instincts, which brought to life a metaphor of relating healthy cells and cancer cells to unhealthy and toxic organizations. Ken believed in me when others thought my ideas were too edgy. Without his trust in me, I would have lost trust in myself, and would not have finished this book.

A very special thanks to Hoop Morgan III, CEO of The Forte Institute, whose partnership for the past thirty years has given me the stamina to stay the course on the Conversational Intelligence journey, knowing that patterns emerge as wisdom grows. Special thanks to the HeartMath Institute, another great Institute of Research and insight, and especially Bruce Cryer and Deborah Rozman, Ph.D., Doc Childre and Dr. Rollin McCraty, whose work has inspired me and expanded my understanding of the Heart/Brain connection.

Conversational Intelligence would not have been written without insights, wisdom and support from my editors, and writing coaches who continued to push me to simplify and clarify my "big thoughts'" so that others can understand my ideas: Art Kleiner, John Fayad, Paul Brown, Peter Gizzardi, Mike Snell, Darren Dahl, Traci Carpenter, Susan Heller, Amy Jameson, Alison Beard (HBR), Herb Addison (Oxford University Press), Phoebe Collins, Helen Whelen (Success TV), and Donna Crovatta. And most of all Judy Katz, who has stuck with me on my book writing projects for over a decade and has given me the confidence and help to express my ideas and thoughts when I was, at times, giving up on myself and Jan Goldstoff, PR, who continues to open my mind to how much the world needs to learn to talk to one another. Also to my

Acknowledgments

animators—Peter Cutler and Seth Kendal, and Joel Marks producer, who helped bring my ideas about moving from Level II to Level III to life by animating my leadership fable—*The Leadership Secret of Gregory Goose*; and special thanks to Ethan Finkelstein and Leslie Shapiro of Color + Information, who did the video trailer for *Conversational Intelligence.*

Conversational Intelligence would not have been written without the trust and support from NAPFA (National Association of Personal Financial Advisors) who challenged me, and my collaborators, Kathy Holland, Ed.D., and Jeff Otten, to immerse their members in a three-day summit on *Conversational Intelligence and the Neuroscience of Trust*—even when "the cake was still baking"—and the book on Conversational Intelligence was not yet complete; and a special thanks to Robin Gemeinhardt and Ellen Turf, then CEO of NAPFA, who believed in our design and energized our co-creation process. Without their trust in my ability to bring complexity down to earth and wisdom into the room, I would not have had the confidence to continue to integrate *science with practice* and make it accessible to so many people.

Conversational Intelligence came one step further into creation when FPA (Financial Planning Association) gave me an opportunity to put my "organizational anthropology" to work in exploring their conversational rituals—and linking them to the neuroscience of bonding and community building—another key anchor that explains Conversational Intelligence from an anthropological perspective. Specifically, I want to thank Rick Miller, PhD, my muse and coach, in helping me bring logic and flow to my thoughts and ideas.

Conversational Intelligence could not have been written without some of my thought partners and friends: Jane Stevenson, a great friend and colleague, continues to lift my thoughts about conversations and continues to encourage me to push the envelope and challenge my own best thinking inside of businesses and beyond the walls of business—to touch the lives of people everywhere who want to join in and have a voice. Kathleen Bollerud-Holland, Ed.D. and Jeff Otten, who have worked with me to ensure that Conversational Intelligence becomes clear enough for every-one around the globe to experience and understand.

Another special thanks to Mary Beth Borgwing, whose partnership over the past seven years has led to the development of C Shift, an excit-ing new application of Conversational Intelligence to expand an organi-zation's ability to develop a healthy risk culture. This body of work is profoundly helping companies become more integrated and capable of elevating the capacity for making risk decisions.

Also, a very special thanks to Julie Anixter, whose has become a spe-cial partner in expanding how Conversational Intelligence takes wings; her ideas for outreach and socializing conversations through social media and is teaching me new dimensions for how 'conversations trans-form the world.' Julie has been a central partner in helping me envi-sion and deliver ways to make Conversational Intelligence accessible to people around the globe conceptually and digitally through Innovation Excellence and other exciting learning media and technology, and has elevated my thinking and helped me define what great partnership is all about. And to Bobbi Van and Mark Monchek, who are helping us build out a platform for C-IQ through TED x NYC and The OPP Lab, and to Mary Ann Somerville who has been a dedicated partner in helping mold and shape our Creating WE Institute Global Enterprises.

A special thanks to Lori Polachek who has brought her energy and enthusiasm to me to expand the Creating WE Institute into the educa-tion field. Her unending passion for understanding the impact of Con-versational Intelligence has enabled us to introduce C-IQ into schools when children are first learning to connect words to ideas, and to impact their ability to speak from their hearts. Lori's energy has brought me new energy, light, and wisdom for how to transform the way we learn, grow and nurture the next generation. Along with Michael Stabile, Ph.D., who adopted my work a decade ago and who has worked with dozens of schools, administrators, and educators to enable Creating WE to become more than a concept of possibility—but a movement in education!

Acknowledgments

And to Pat Mastandrea, CEO of The Cheyenne Group, who continues to believe in me and my work and encourages and pushes me to keep going, to keep challenging, and to keep writing about what success looks like in business, education, and globally in the world. To Jane Wesman Public Relations who continues to fuel 'my platform and challenge my voice.' To Karen Pinkman of Jobplex, Inc. who enabled me to think out load with her when my voice ran dray. And to all the media who would allow me to say what was on my mind when I was still "in the journey"— Joanne Lublin, WSJ; Rebecca Surran, Channel 12; CBS News, NBC, Fox, ABC and so many others. What great partners to inspire this journey!

Conversational Intelligence comes to life when my clients embrace the frameworks and ideas and introduce them and experiment with them in their organizations. Jane Stevenson, who, as the head of the CEO and Board practice at Korn Ferry, is partnering with me to bring Conversational Intelligence into organizations. Together, along with Peter Thies, we have been *pushing the envelope* on how to engage large organizations, such as Target Corporation, in expanding their capacity for Conversational Intelligence. In that spirit, a particular special thanks to Gregg Steinhafel, CEO of Target and Kathee Tesija, Target's EVP of Merchandizing and Supply Chain, along with her team who voraciously and profoundly engaged with Conversational Intelligence at the highest level that I have seen a team embrace this body of work. They not only captured the power of Conversation Intelligence amongst their team, they engaged with their direct reports to apply this wisdom as well— creating an opening for strategic transformational conversations to live inside of their cross functional teams. Seeing a team as incredible as the Target team apply the principles and practices of Level III Conversations with such exquisite skill was profound and inspiring—and I will be forever grateful for their commitment to this work.

In addition, another special thanks to Joe Bonito, a long-time colleague and supporter of this work through his tenure at Pfizer, Coach, and now Bank of America, along with Jim Czupil also from Bank of

Acknowledgments

America, who believed in Conversational Intelligence and engaged us to work with leaders to strengthen their corporate culture and expand their executives' abilities to positively influence their organization and customers. Also, I'd like to thank AIG, specifically Gayle Kennedy-Hill, and Maggie Williams, as well as the other valued executives at AIG, who have made Conversational Intelligence a part of the coaching experience for many of the company's senior executives. Most of all a special thanks to Joan Lawrence-Ross, the Chief Learning Officer at AIG, who has been a devoted colleague for over a few decades, has made this work available to Citi, AXA Equitable and now AIG. And a uniquely special thanks to Frank Palantoni, who has taken my work to Novartis, Gerber, Central Garden and Pet, and continues to bring me into his work to work with him on his challenges. Frank inspires me to think, experiment, test my ideas, and stretch my thinking in all of his many endeavors.

Conversational Intelligence was a journey over three decades of client engagements. Each added the opportunity to experiment with new approaches, new practices, and new conversational rituals to see which ones had the sustaining power to prove that they were impactful and valuable enough to transfer to the next generation of executives within their organizations. Some of these clients include: Angela Ahrendts, CEO of Burberry who has supported and encouraged me, and allowed me to be a part of her leadership journey and most recently the global transformation of Burberry; Donna Karan whom I worked with closely for a number of years during the transformation of Donna Karan International into a more integrated design organization; Mary Wang, now president of DNKY, who also embraced Conversational Intelligence through her tenure at DK and Coach; Steve Sadov, CEO of Clairol and now Sachs; and Paul Carlucci, Chairman of News American Marketing; Gerritt Schipper, CEO of RDC; Kathie Duff-Wilson and Bill Burns at Emery Worldwide; Lucy Nelson at Revlon; Carol Woods at Champion International; Bob Fuller from UST and Siemens Medical; Terry Dockins from Boehringer Ingelheim; Mila Baker and Phil Sleeman at Pfizer; Stan Juozaitus at Lipton and

Acknowledgments

Unilever; Maureen Bies, Valerie Calabro and their HR teams at Veeco Instruments; Amy Margolis at Merrill Lynch; Bronwen Bastone at Knight Capital; John Bennett, PhD at the University of Charlotte; Benjy Karsch at CIGNA; Anna Bakst, CEO of Michael Kors; Susan Sachs at Cooke and Company; Marcia Goldstein at Weil Gottshal & Manges; Sara Littauer and Lori Martin at Wilmer Hale; Randy White, PhD, and Sandy Shullman, PhD, at EDG Associates; Kathy Kavanagh and Saj Samuel at PwC; Peter Thies at The River Group; Nancy Parsons at WorldTravel BTI; Cathleen Raffaeli at Cardean; Caroline Vanderlip at Shared Book; Steve Elias at Louisville Bedding and Rob Rudy at Standard Pro; Toni Bales, Bill Robinson at Avon; Barrett Brown, Melissa Galligan at Viking Global Investors; Cheryl Rathbun at Citi; Jill Hampton at Bombardier; Bob Lutz, Retired Vice Chairman of GM; Allen & Overy; Henry Kravis, George Roberts, Bob Gottlieb and Dean Nelson at KKR; Scudder Fowler of the Liminal Group; Damien Dernacourt, CEO of John Hardy; Open Door; Novartis; Michael Frieze, Chairman of Gordon Brothers Group; Jack Sosiak of Exide technologies; Craig Mulhhauser, CEO of Celestica; Tracey Riese of Tracy Riese and Associates; Estee Lauder;; Russell Investments; Forbes; Reed Business & Reed Elsevier; Labor Ready; J & J; JPMorgan; Gerber; American Cyanamid; De Beers; General Dynamics; Lockheed Martin and all the other incredible clients who were willing to experiment with me in this incredibly fascinating field of Conversational Intelligence. Another very special thanks to colleagues who have been partners over the years. Bobby Little, of PDI, who helped me discover how much I love coaching. Peyton Daniel from LHH, who has partnered with me for over a decade and a half, and enabled me to introduce Conversational Intelligence as a Coaching Practice to so many wonderful clients. And to TEC and Vistage International enabled me to work with so many incredible CEOs over the past decade. Without these courageous and effective executives this work would remain on the pages of my books— instead it's empowered leaders around the globe to lead better.

Conversational Intelligence would not have been possible without the

Acknowledgments

support of all the members of the Creating WE Institute, who have lived this journey of discovery with me for almost a decade, and who have shared their great wisdom and insights throughout the full extent of the learning journey. All of our conversations over the past few years served as treasured gifts to nurture our humanity and patience, as we worked to put words to a science that was emerging right in front of our eyes.

They include Marla Emery and Rhonda York, co-directors of CWI Charlotte; Rex Jung, PhD; Richard Glaser, PhD; Peg Aldridge; Michelle Boos-Stone; Jan Goldstoff; Bud Bilanich, EdD; Debra Pearce-McCall, PhD; Mary Ann Somerville; Cindy Tortorici; Lori Polechek; Catherine Mullally; Jane Hewson; Jon Entine; Brian Penry; Si Alhir; Zeinab Hussein; Abdallah Hussein Khamis; Barbara Biziou; Robert Galinsky; Geoff Grenert, MBA; Donna Riechmann, PhD; Jo Washington; Joan Heffler; Deborah Dumaine; Louise van Rhyn, EdD; Dale Kramer-Cohen, MBA; Deborah Hicks-Midanek; Coley Bailey; Denise Harrington; Debra Dumaine; Elizabeth Glaser; Victor Rosansky; Susanne Atkins; Lisa Giruzzi; Katinka Nicou; Whit Raymond, M.Ed; Stan Labovitz; Monica Caviglia; Sandra Gil; Louis Alloro; Nancy Ring; Zandra Harris, PhD; Robert Fuller, MA; Alan Booth; Deborah Garand; Kathy Duff-Wilson; Christine Lewis Varley; Ben Dattner, PhD; Nancy Snell; Karen Spofford, MBA; Erica Dhawan; Stephanie Eidelman; Kathleen Bollerud-Holland, EdD, Jeff Otten; Bryan Mattimore of The Growth Engine; Sheri Boyd of Boyd Solutions; Deanna Brown; and Fernando Natalici.

And to the **Platinum Group**, a cadre of colleagues who support each other's work and engage in productive, generative, and co-creating conversations to expand each other's work including: Stan Labovitz; George Labovitz; Dick Kimball; Barbara Annis; Hubert St Onge; Mike Jay; and Tim Maroney.

Last but not least, *Conversational Intelligence* is also dedicated to my team of extraordinary colleagues who are helping take this work outside of the four walls of our businesses to help launch our global Conversational Intelligence initiative called **Conversations that Transform His-**

tory which will be launched through a partnership with the National Constitution Center in Philadelphia and The Creating WE Institute for Global Initiative. The NCC colleagues who are enabling this idea to come to life are Jeffery Rosen, CEO; Vince Stango; COO; Ray Salva; Margaret Cronan; Alison Young; Lauren Saul; as well as Paul Gluck and Don Heller from Temple University; Louisa Hanshew, Rebecca Weidensaul and Richard Kopp from Drexel University, Julie Anixter; Joan Holman; Lynda Koster; Frank Migliorelli; Karen Parella; with a very special thanks to a long-time friend and colleague, Tom Rosenwald, who continues to step into my life when I'm working on something with potential, and shines the light on how to bring every project to life even when others have passed it by...he breathes life into potential!

Conversational Intelligence emerged more clearly in my mind when I was doing my graduate studies. I could not have produced this book without the inspired research and teachings, as well as the incredible support of professors from Temple University, Drexel University, Harvard University, Fairfield University and University of Pennsylvania who believed, as I did that at the intersection of science and art, or anthropology, psychology and linguistics, was un-mined wisdom that could transform the world.

Conversational Intelligence has been inspired by the ongoing support from Allen Sabinson, Dean of the Westphal College at Drexel University and Louisa Hanshew, Assistant Dean who enabled me to collaborate with the talented professors, staff and students at the Westphal College. Also special thanks to Temple University's Chancellor Richard Englert, and Ashley Lomery, Executive Director of Leadership Giving who have ensured I speak with everyone at Temple who can help us build collaborative partnerships within and without the University; and specifically to Rebecca Weidensaul PhD, Associate Dean of Students, and to Richard Kopp, Director Student Leadership Development & Traditions.

Special thanks to the neuroscientists whose work had such an influence on my thinking and on the development of the Conversational Intelligence framework:

Rex Jung PhD, Assistant Professor of Neurosurgery at the University

Acknowledgments

of Mexico who is one of our founding members of the Creating WE Institute; Bruce McEwen PhD, Alfred E. Mirsky Professor and Head, Harold and Margaret Milliken Hatch Laboratory of Neuroendocrinology at The Rockefeller University; Angelika Dimoka PhD, Associate Professor at the Fox School of Business and Director of the Center for Neural Decision Making, Temple University; Paul A. Pavlou, PhD, Professor of Management Information Systems, Marketing, and Strategic Management, Fox School of Business at Temple University; Ralph Young, PhD, Professor of History at Temple University; John Bargh, PhD, Professor of Psychology, Yale University; Stephen Porges, PhD, Research Professor of Psychology at Northeastern University and Adjunct Professor of Psychiatry at The University of North Carolina; Sue Carter, PhD, Research Professor of Psychology at Northeastern University and Adjunct Professor of Psychiatry at The University of North Carolina ; Jessie Williams, PhD; Uri Hasson, PhD, Assistant Professor of Psychology at Princeton University; Paul Zak, PhD, a pioneer in the field of neuro-economics; and many, many others who have moved our insights about Conversational Intelligence further along.

Last but not least, a special thanks to the Qualtrics team: Ryan Smith, CEO, Caleb Wilkins, and Jeff Harvey whose support and help in enabling our TRUST Assessment and Creating WE Index to be available to so many people; and to Stan Labovitz, CEO of Infotool, who enabled my research on the DNA of Leadership which led to the framework for Conversational Intelligence.

To get to the next level of greatness, depends
on the quality of the culture,
which depends on the quality of the relationships,
which depends on the quality of the conversations.
Everything happens through conversations!

INDEX

A

accountability, 127, 181
  Make Up Game and, 144–145
adrenaline, 90
"Advocate and Inquire" interactions, 69–70
aggression, 40, 73
agility, conversational, 117–135
  dashboards and, 118–120
  rebuilding trust and, 134–135
  reframing, refocusing, redirecting in, 122–125
  road map for building, 125–134
  teaching, 120–123
Ahrendts, Angela, 154–158, 160–161
alignment
  of intentions with impact, 101, 104–107
  transforming anger into, 143–145
amygdala
  Conversational Dashboard and, 35–37
  in desire to win, 7–9
  distrust and, 24–25
  hijacking by, 26–28
  LEARN exercise and, 143
  overcoming triggers from, 28–29
  refocusing to promote trust, 126–127
  reward vs. punishment and, 74
  speed of response from, 42, 76–77
  threat response by, 75–77
Ancona, Deborah, 91–92
anger, transforming into alignment, 143–145
anterior cingulate cortex (ACC), 4–5

AOL, 176
appreciation, 84
ARC of Engagement, 121–122
argument, designed for, 89–91
aspirations
  mental "movies" and, 38–39
  understanding, 129–130
aspiring conversations, 162, 163–164
assumptions
  about meaning, 66
  about memory, 65
  blind spots from, 64–67
  heart responses to testing, 54
  "I to WE" shift and, 57
  Ladder of Conclusions and, 41–42
  testing, 47, 51–52, 92
avoidance, xviii

B

Back to the Future exercise, 147–149
Bailey, Christopher, 156–157
Balkam, Stephen, 175–181
Bargh, John, 108, 110–111
barriers, removing, 180–181
belonging, 133
  fear of exclusion and, 173
  human need for, 158–159,
    195–196
betrayal, xviii
  becoming someone else from, 40

Index

betrayal (*continued*)
  distrust and, 34
  oppositional response to, 51–52
biases, 3–4
  mental "movies" and, 6–7
blind spots, 63–67
  monitoring, 68–70
Blue Exhibit, 187–191
body language. *See* nonverbal communication
Boehringer Ingelheim, xxii–xxv, xxvii
Bravo, Rose Marie, 155
breakdowns, conversational, 64–67
bridging, 143–145
Burberry, 154–158, 160–161

C
Caring Effect, 84
catalytic questions, 67, 68
catecholamine, 40
Center for Neural Decision Making, 24
certainty, 185–186
chairs, hard vs. soft, 110–111
change, 153–154
  buy-in to, 196–197
  conversational rituals for, 194–199
  creating space for, 197–198
  creating space for co-creation in, 188–191
  creating space for new reality in, 187–188
  exciting, 183–184
  fear of, 178
  getting unstuck in, 191–194
  intelligence and, 186–187
  mind-set and, 195–196
  seeing differently, 183–186
  as threat, 160–161
  transformational, 201–204
Clairol, 92–99
Clairol News Network, 96
coaching, 4
Co-creating Conversations, xx, 162, 163
  brain rewiring through, 80–81
  in change, 188–191
  change and, 197–198
  at Lockheed, 192–193
  mind-set for, 106–107
  rituals in, 63

cognitive responses, speed of, 42
coherence, 52–53, 74–75, 79, 82
  LEARN exercise and, 143
collaboration
  at Clairol, 98
  conflict and, 139–141
  oxytocin and, 77
  in teams, 170–172
collective intelligence, 161–162
comfort, 110–111
commitment, 181
common ground, finding, 123–124
competitiveness, 169
compliance, 171
conclusions, 42–43
Conclusions, Ladder of Conclusions, 41–42,
    114–115, 193
confidence
  communicating, 84
  inspiring, 85
conflict
  aversion to, 170
  blind spots and, 64–67
  co-creation from, 139–141
  engagement during, 137–139
  fear triggered by, 26
  healthy, 171
  neurochemical responses to, 40
conformity, 172–173
confrontation, 54–56
connectivity
  failure to achieve, 7
  heart in, 5–6
  neuroscience of, 14
contact, moment of, 12–13
context, 49–50
  eliminating fear with, 174
  priming and, 109–110, 111–114
  reframing and, 123–124
Conversational Dashboard, 35–37
  assessing conversations with, 115–116, 122
  at Clairol, 93–94
  gauging results with, 68–70
  reframing with, 122–123
Conversational Intelligence
  assessing, 115–116

Index

at Clairol, 92–99
cultivating, xxi
five brains in, 73–85
harvesting, 81–83
in Internet Content Rating Association, 175–181
learnability of, xviii
mastering, 198–199
neurochemistry and, xix
premise of, xix
teams and, 167–182
what it is, xx–xxi
Conversational Intelligence Matrix, 71
conversations
blind spots in, 63–67
desire to win and, 8–9
feel-good vs. feel-bad, 4–5
having uncomfortable, 29–30
history shaping, 202–204
intentions vs. impact in, 3–4
learning from our worst, 3–19
mental "movies" during, 6–7, 27–28, 117, 134
neurochemistry triggered by, 5–6 (See also neuroscience)
positional, xx
power of, xvii
rituals in, 61–63
shaping for success, 61–72
space for, xxviii–xxix
cooperation, 102–103, 119
co-regulation, 116
core values, 129
cortisol, 35, 40
fear and, 73
fear reduction and, 117
response to lowering, 82–83
shelf life of, 104
Coyle, Dan, 145–146
Creating WE (Glaser), 13–14
Creating WE Institute, 29–30, 73–74
Creating We process, 11–13
creativity, 171, 172–173
culture, organizational, 66–67
at Burberry, 156–157
co-creating meaning in, 91–92

conversational rituals for changing, 194–199
in decision making, 172–173
uncertainty about fitting in, 129–131

D
dashboards, 118–120
decision-making, 154, 172–173
deconstructing conversations, 13–15, 23
defensiveness, 44
in team storming stage, 169–170
uncertainty and, 129–131
DHEA, 117
Dimoka, Angelika, xxix, 24, 154
discovery questions, 67
disengaging, 114–115
dishonesty, xviii
distrust, xviii
betrayal and, 34
blind spots about, 65
brain responses to, 24–25
heart rate and, 75
intentions and, 21–23
of leaders, 39
maintenance of, 28–29
moving to trust from, 33–57
neurochemistry of, 40
old memories and, 27–28
power of, 11–13
reality gaps and, 10–11
ripple effects of, 157–158
Third Eye skills and, 105–107
uncertainty and, 25, 130
diversity, 131
DNA of Leadership, The (Glaser), 13–14
dopamine, 29–30, 40
confidence and, 85
fear and, 103–104
in persuasion, 64–65
Double-Clicking exercise, 138–139, 140, 141–142
down-regulating, 179–180
dramatization of messages, xxvii–xxviii

E
Eisenberger, Naomi, 83
emotion. See also distrust; fear

emotion (*continued*)
  at Burberry, 156–157
  genetic regulation of, 82–83
  labeling interactions with, 42
  mindfulness of, xxviii–xxix
  understanding, 46
empathy, xxviii, 35
  asking questions and, 68
  blind spots about, 65
  mirror neurons and, 65
  trust and, 49
endorphins, 83, 85
engagement
  ARC of, 121–122
  in conflict, 137–139
  relationship building and, 129
  rituals in, 64
  rules of, for trust, 30–31, 112–113
  storytelling and, 196–197
  supportive, xxviii
  triggering, 111–114
environment changes, 108–110,
    110–111
  co-regulating, 116
  for trust and openness, 113–114
exclusion, fear of, 173
executive brain. *See* prefrontal cortex
exercises
  Back to the Future, 147–149
  Double-Clicking, 138–139, 140,
    141–142
  LEARN, 143
  Looking Back to Look Forward,
    146–147
  Make Up Game, 144–145
  Rules of Engagement, 112–113
Exide Technologies, 89
expectations, 24–25
  dashboards and, 120
  limbic brain and, 81
experiences
  limbic brain memories of, 50
  mental "movies" and, 38–39
Experiment in International Living,
    183–184
Experimentors, 36, 126

expressing conversations, 162, 165
expression, 102–103, 119

F
failure
  fear of
    failure to connect and, 7–9
    leaders and, 39
    primitive responses to, 37–38
  reframing, 186
fairness, 102–103, 119
Fast Company, 155
fear
  blind spots about, 65
  change and, 153–154
  in conflict, 26
  of exclusion, 173
  of failure, connecting and, 7–9
  phantom, 178
  priming the pump and, 107–109
  reducing, 117
  refocusing on transparency, 126–127
  reptilian brain and, 81
  in teams, 173–174
  Third Eye skills and, 105–107
  transforming into trust, 29
  trustworthiness and, 103–104
  visualizing success and, 178–179
fear networks, 44
feedback, 43
  eliminating fear with, 174
  relationship building and, 129
  sharing, 97
  trust/distrust and, 24–25
fight–flight–freeze response, 12, 40, 76
fitting in, 50, 129–131
FORCES, 102–104, 119
forming stage, 167–169
FOXP2 gene, 82–83
fronto-insular (FI) cortex, 4–5

G
generating conversations, 162, 164–165
genetic change, 82–83
Global Teen Leaders, 203–204
Groupthink, 39, 54–55

Index

refocusing on truth telling and, 133–134
Groysberg, Boris, 154
gut instincts, 4–5

H

Harold and Margaret Milliken Hatch
  Laboratory of Neuroendocrinology, 74
Hasson, Uri, 80–81
heart responses, 5–6
  coherence, 52–53, 74–75, 82
  heart brain, 48–49, 52–54, 75, 78
  in sync vs. out of sync, 26
honesty. *See* truth telling
humanizing conversations, 162, 163
humor, 115, 145

I

IBM, 176
ICRA, 175–181
influence, 188–191
insights, 142–143
  harvesting, 145–149
instincts
  gaining mastery over, 14
  gut, 4–5
  as invisible dashboards, 118–120
  overcoming, 28–29
  vital, 14, 101–104
Institute of Heart Math, 52–53
Instituto Americano, 201–202
intelligence, collective, 161–162
intentions
  aligning with impact, 101, 104–107
  distrust and, 21–23
  I-centric leadership and, 16–18
  impact vs., 3–4, 9–10
  in priming, 111
  Third Eye skills and, 10, 57, 104–107
  transparency of, 47–48
interaction dynamics, 79–81, 98
interaction patterns, 14
Interbrand, 155
Internet Content Rating Association (ICRA),
  175–181
"I to WE" shift, 56–57

J

judgment, 48–49
Jung, Rex, 73

K

Korzybski, Alfred, xxiii

L

labeling, 156–157
Ladder of Conclusions, 41–42, 193
  disengaging from, 114–115
leaders and leadership
  addiction to being right and, 15–16
  asking "what if" questions and,
    29–30, 131
  at Burberry, 154–158
  Caring Effect and, 84
  changing tactics for, 87–99
  co-creating meaning and, 91–92
  eliminating fear in, 174–175
  I-centric, 16–18
  intention vs. impact of, 106–107
  loss of power of, 39
  "my way or the highway," 39
  self-awareness for, 44
  stuck at Level I, 87–89
  with trust, foundations for, 153–166
  uncomfortable conversations and, 29–30
  WE-centric, 18–19
LEARN exercise, 143
learning
  creating opportunities for, 127
  from doing, 39
Level I conversations, 69
  change and, 186
  at Clairol, 94–95
  stuck in, 87–89
Level II conversations, 69–70
  change and, 186
  getting unstuck from, 191–194
  stuck in, 89–91
Level III conversations, xxii
  change and, 186–187
  in everyday life, 194–199
  evolving insights/wisdom from, 142–143

227

Index

Level III conversations (*continued*)
  laying foundations for, 153–166
  possibilities in, 91–92
  priming for, 101–116
  questions in, 67–68
  seven vital, 162–166
  Third Eye skills and, 104–107
  toolkit for, 137–149
  transformation through, 70
level setting, 119–120, 149
Lieberman, Matt, 83
limbic brain, 50, 78
listening, xxv–xxvii
  coherence and, 80
  conversational agility and, 118
  nonjudgmental, 65
  trust and, 80
Lockheed Martin, 191–194
logic, power of, 196–197
Looking Back to Look Forward, 13–15,
    145–149
Lutz, Bob, 88–89

M
Make Up Game, 144–145
manipulation, 111
McEwen, Bruce S., 73–75
meaning
  assumptions about, 66
  co-creating, 91–92
  deconstructing conversations for,
    13–14
  Ladder of Conclusions and, 41–42
  making of, 11, 148
  validating shared, 66
Mehrabian, Albert, 80
mental "movies," 6–7, 23
  activation of old, 27–28
  fear reduction and, 117
  sharing to remove reality gaps, 134
Mercier, Hugo, 90
Microsoft, 176
mindfulness, xxviii–xxix
mind-sets, changing, 195–196
mirror neurons, xxvii, 49, 65
Morris, Michael, 172

N
Nasser, Jacques, 88
National Constitution Center, 204
navigating conversations, 162, 164
negative thought loops, 117
negotiation, 114–115
neocortex, 51, 78
  Third Eye skills and, 104–107
neural coupling, 80–81
neural network, 4–5
neuroplasticity, 82–83
neuroscience, xix
  on argument, 89–91
  brain landscape and, 75–77
  Conversational Dashboard and, 35–37
  of Conversational Intelligence, 83
  on conversational neurochemistry, 29–30
  on conversational triggers, 5–6
  of desire to win, 7–8
  on distrust, 24–25, 103–104
  heart brain, 48–49, 52–54, 75
  on how conversations shape our brains,
    13–15
  on labeling, 156–157
  Level III conversations and,
    xxii
  on master and slave responses, 81–83
  of mental "movies," 38–39
  neuro coupling and, 80–81
  of our five brains, 73–85
  on relationship building, 128
  reticular activating system, xxvi–xxvii
  of sharing stories of mutual success, 131
  of success, 51
  on temperature and character assessment,
    108–109
  on trust, xxviii, 4–5
  on trust vs. distrust, 26–28, 40
  on truth telling, 133
  of understanding others, 49–50
  of WE, xxvi, 35
neurotransmitters, 79, 85. *See also* oxytocin
New Wave Entertainment, 120–121
nonverbal communication, 11, 77,
    79–81
norming stage, 170–171

Index

O

open-ended questions, 67–68
openness, 113–114
  facilitative effects of, 196
  in teams, 172
orbitofrontal cortex, 25
organizational anthropology, 184–185
ownership, 102–103, 119
oxytocin, 29–30, 37
  happiness from, 77
  trust and, 49
  uncertainty and, 112

P

pain vs. pleasure, 173–174
Partnering Conversations, 48
partnerships. *See also* relationships
  brain design for, 25
  refocusing from Groupthink toward, 133–134
passive-aggressive behaviors, 170
pattern interrupts, 145
Pavlou, Paul, 154
performance reviews, 127
performing stage, 171–172
personalities, conflict between, 137–139
perspective, 198
  assumption about others', 64–65
  finding common ground and, 123–124
  harvesting new, 145–149
  leadership and, 16–18
  understanding others', 49–50, 97
persuasion, 64–65
pleasure vs. pain, 173–174
politics, conflict from, 137–139
Polyvagal Theory, 75
Porges, Stephen, 75
positional conversations, xx
power
  conflict and, 137–140
  influence and, 188–191
  over vs. with, xiii, 55
  refocusing to create relationships, 127–129
  sharing in teams, 170–171
  us vs. them, 54–55
praise, 85

predictability, 185–186
prefrontal cortex, xxi, 78
  activating, 28–29
  amygdala vs., 8–9
  Conversational Dashboard and, 35–37
  hijacking of, 76
  in making sense of reality, 133–134
  trust and, 24–25, 74
priming, 101–116
  beforehand, 111–114
  at Burberry, 158
  during conversations, 114–115
  environment and, 108–110
  at Lockheed, 193–194
primitive brain. *See* amygdala
problem solving, applying old solutions to, 38–39
Procter & Gamble, 92, 99
productivity, 173–174
provocative questions, 67

Q

questions
  asking smart, xxv
  asking "what if," 29–30, 131
  catalytic, 67, 68
  discovery, 67
  five hardwired, 84–85
  open-ended, 67–68
  provocative, 67
  statements in disguise vs., 62–63

R

rapport, xxv–xxvii, 109–110, 131
reality, xx
  blind spots about interpreting, 65, 66–67
  change and, 187–188
  dashboards and, 120
  expectations vs., 24–25
  map vs. territory of, xxii
  mental "movies" of, 6–7, 23
  sharing, 83
  trust vs. distrust and views of, 159–160
reality gaps, 10–11
  bridging, 66–67
  at Clairol, 97–98
  closing, 72

Index

reality gaps (*continued*)
 distrust and, 23
 refocusing on truth telling and, 133–134
real-plays, 62–63
reciprocity, 102–103, 119
Recreational Software Advisory Council, 175
redirecting, 122–123, 125
refocusing, 122–123, 124–125
 from fear to transparency, 126–127
 from power to relationship building,
  127–129
 on shared success, 131–132
reframing, xxiv, 122–124
 change, 183–186
 resistance, 194–195
relationships, xix
 being in sync in, 26
 building, 48–49
 customer-centric, at Clairol, 96–97
 Double-Clicking and, 141–142
 heart responses to, 54
 human need for, 82, 83
 "I to WE" shift and, 56
 moment of contact in, xxiv
 partnerships, 25
 refocusing from power to, 127–129
 resetting for trust, 30–31
 task vs., xxiv
 trust in, 45–46
 turning adversarial into partnerships, xxii–xxv
 turning anger into alignment in, 143–145
 unconventional, nurturing, 157
 us vs. them, 54–55
reptilian brain, 78
resistance, 194–195
Resistors, 36, 123
 turning into Experimentors, 125–134
respect, 48–49
responsibility, accepting, 144–145
reticular activating system (RAS), xxvii,
  124–125
rightness
 addiction to, 15–16, 64–65
 designed to seek, 89–91
 proving, of our conclusions, 42–43
risk, 185

rituals, 61, 62
 blind spots and, 63–67
 during change, 185
 at Clairol, 95–96
 co-creating, 72
 culture and, 66–67
 ineffective, 62–63
Rizzolatti, Giacomo, 65
Rules of Engagement exercise, 112–113

S
Sadove, Steve, 96
safety, 14
 heart responses to, 53
 human need for, 195–196
 at ICRA, 179
scripts, 81
seating arrangements, 113–114
self-awareness, 4, 30. *See also* Third Eye skills
 in leadership, 44
 leadership and, 166
 priming and, 110
 Third Eye skills and, 106–107
self-expression, 131, 162, 165
self-protection, 26–28
self-regulation, 117
Senge, Peter, 91
sense making, 91. *See also* meaning
serotonin, 29–30, 85
"Share and Discover" dynamics, 70. *See also*
  Level III conversations
sharing
 human need for, 56, 91–92
 insights and wisdom, 142–143
skepticism, 194–195
Skeptics, 123
 turning into Experimentors, 125–134
Slind, Michael, 154
sociability, 82, 83
Sperber, Dan, 90
Star Skills, xxvi–xxix
status, 102–103, 119
storming stage, 169–170
storytelling, 196–197
stuttering, 202–203
success, xxii

Index

contagiousness of, xxvii–xxviii
conversational rituals for, 194–199
conversations celebrating, 162, 165–166
creating vision of shared, 97
Double-Clicking exercise and, 138–139
"I to WE" shift and, 57
looking back to look forward and, 145–149
mapping, 140
neuroscience on, 185
reinforcing, xxv–xxvii
removing barriers to, 180–181
shaping conversations for, 61–72
shared, 46, 50–51
   creating space for, 190
   eliminating fear with, 174
   heart responses to, 54
   in Level III conversations, 92
   refocusing on, 131–132
   sharing stories of mutual, 131
   visualizing, 178–179
support, 84, 85
synchronization
   heart responses to, 26
   LEARN exercise and, 143
synchronizing conversations, 162, 165–166

T

The Talent Code (Coyle), 145–146
Talk, Inc. (Groysberg & Slind), 154
teams, 167–182
   at Burberry, 156–157
   conformity in, 172–173
   development stages of, 167
   diversity in, 131
   forming stage of, 169, 167
   ICRA, 175–181
   norming stage of, 170–171
   overcoming fear in, 173–174
   performing stage of, 171–172
   storming stage of, 169–170
   value of individuals in, 181
TEDxTeen, 204
Telecom, 176
"Tell and Ask" interactions, 69
Tell–Sell–Yell Syndrome, 8–9, 17,
   87–89

temperature, character assessment and,
   108–109, 110–111
template genes, 82
testosterone, 40, 73, 90
Third Eye skills, 10, 57, 104–107
   Double-Clicking, 138–139
   phantom fear and, 178
threats
   amygdala response to, 26–28, 75–77
   changing responses to, 28–29
   making transparent, 47
   priming the pump and, 107–109
360-degree interviews, 44
Three Dot Dash, 203–204
tone of voice, 80
transcription genes, 82
transformational change, 201–204
transparency, 45, 47–48
   about fears, 179
   at Clairol, 96
   eliminating fear with, 174
   facilitative effects of, 196
   heart responses to, 53
   "I to WE" shift and, 56
   in Level III conversations, 92
   refocusing to promote, 126–127
trust, xxviii–xxix, 21–31
   blind spots about, 65
   brain responses to, 24–25
   connection and, 82
   Conversational Dashboard and,
      69–70
   decision-making and, 154
   in the future, 148–149
   gut instincts in, 4–5
   heart energy in, 48–49
   heart rate and, 75
   importance of, 11–13
   intentions and, 21–23
   interaction dynamics in, 79–81
   "I to WE" shift and, 56–57
   Ladder of Conclusions and, 41–42
   in Level III, 105
   measuring, 83
   moving from distrust to, 33–57
   neurochemistry of, 40, 74

trust *(continued)*
  neuroscience of, xxviii, 4–5
  rebuilding, 44–45, 134–135
  redirecting to promote, 125
  refocusing to promote, 126–127
  reframing to promote, 123–124
  resetting relationships for, 30–31
  sensing trustworthiness, 103–104
  shaking hands and, 111–112
  shaping space for, 113–114
  sustaining, 28
  Third Eye skills and, 105–107
  triggering, 111–114
  uncertainty and, 130
  Vital Instincts on, 101–104
  vulnerability and, 28
TRUST Checklist, 95–96
"Trust Hormone Associated with Happiness"
  (Zak), 77
TRUST Model, 45–52
  eliminating fear with, 174–175
  heart brain and, 53–54
trust networks, 44–45, 54, 153
truth telling, 47, 51–52
  at Clairol, 97–98
  eliminating fear with, 175
  heart responses to, 54
  "I to WE" shift and, 57
  in Level III conversations, 92
Tuckman, Bruce, 167–168

U
uncertainty
  leaders and, 39
  reducing in Level III, 140–141
  refocusing on understanding from,
    129–131
  removing, 112
  in team forming stage, 167–169
  trust/distrust and, 25

understanding, 46, 49–50
  heart responses to, 54
  "I to WE" shift and, 56–57
  in Level III conversations, 92
  refocusing uncertainty to, 129–131
Union Carbide, 62–63, 66–67
United States Constitution, 204
up-regulating, 179–180

V
VENs, 4–5
vision, of shared success, 50–51
Vital Instincts, 14, 101–104
von Economo, Constantin, 4–5

W
WAFF, 203–204
Watt, Donald, 183
We Are Family Foundation (WAFF),
  203–204
WE-centric perspective, 16–18
  change and, 186–187
  understanding others in, 130–131
"what if" questions, 29–30, 131
Williams, Lawrence E., 108
winning
  addition to being right and, 15–16
  desire for and failure to connect, 7–9
wisdom, 142–143
  harvesting, 145–149
word choice, xxix, 80
  intention vs. impact with, 9–10
  power of, 28–29
WPP/BrandZ, 155

Y
You Stupid Idiot syndrome, 90–91

Z
Zak, Paul, 77